D1613164

Dear Psychiatrist . . .

Do Child Care Specialists Understand?

Jennie Roberts

DISCARDED

Ⓛ

The Lutterworth Press

Cambridge

£9.99
N

A 010714

WM 8 24
MAIDSTONE HOSPITAL
POSTGRADUATE CENTRE
THE LIBRARY

21430

The Lutterworth Press
P.O. Box 60
Cambridge
CB1 2NT

British Library Cataloguing in Publication Data:
A catalogue record is available from the British Library.

ISBN 0 7188 2935 2

Copyright © Jennie Roberts 1995

The rights of Jennie Roberts to be identified as the
Author of this work have been asserted by her in accordance with the
Copyright Designs and Patents Act 1988.

All rights reserved. No part of this publication may be reproduced,
stored in a retrieval system or transmitted in any form or by any means,
electronic, mechanical, photocopying, recording or otherwise,
without the prior permission in writing of the Publisher.

PE S017

THE LIBRARY
POSTGRADUATE CENTRE
MAIDSTONE HOSPITAL

Printed in Great Britain by
Redwood Books Ltd

To 'Tom'

PREFACE

Eleven years ago I wrote an account of our moderately handicapped son's development 0-15 years and of the extra handicap he suffered through bullying and ridicule. I also tried to show how unhelpful attitudes from some members of the medical, teaching, psychological and psychiatric professions had added yet further difficulties for him. Being unable to find a publisher for this fairly straightforward biography, I somewhat daringly opted for a second and completely unconventional form – and this time was successful. Baroness Warnock's Foreword was written for the first account (the straight biography). As the same points are made in this second account the Foreword is still used with just one or two small alterations. Baroness Warnock has also added a postscript.

FOREWORD

The story of Tom is fascinating and illuminating in equal proportions.

One of the main purposes of the Report on Children with Special Needs (1978), and of the subsequent 1981 Education Act, was to take proper account of the vast differences between different children with learning difficulties; and Tom emerges from these pages as his own person, an individual of wit and courage, with patchy talents, sensitive feelings, and enormous difficulties to overcome in adapting to the world.

The story is of how his adaptation has been affected by others; by his parents, and the professionals with whom he and they were involved. The lessons are clear enough. First and most important, it is essential that teachers should, in their training, come to realize the variety of obstacles that may stand in the way of education for children whose needs are special, the greatest obstacle of all being a feeling of failure and hopelessness. *All* teachers need to learn that this feeling of failure may come from the bullying and ridicule of contemporaries, or from a crass failure of imagination on the part of some teachers themselves. Without such training, and a willingness to put it into practice, the policy of integrating handicapped children into ordinary classes may be a disaster.

The second lesson is that, if things are to go well, there must be cooperation among the professionals themselves. This means that teachers, doctors and social workers must trust each other, believe each other, and write proper reports to each other. It is a tall order; but it is essential if the child himself is not to suffer.

Third there is a lesson to be learned about parents. In the Report we boldly entitled one chapter 'Parents as Partners'. We knew this to be provocative, but we meant it. The parents of a handicapped child are in a position to know him in a way that no one else can. They know what he can do, what flusters him, what he will regard as unjust or humiliating. Too often these parents are treated by the professionals as the source of certain factual information about childhood illnesses and position among siblings, but otherwise as fools; or, worse, as pig-headed, over-protective or over-ambitious villains. All professionals are equally guilty; among all of them such attitudes are sometimes to be found, though doubtless for rather different reasons. And so the history of the relationships between Tom's parents and the professionals should be compulsory reading for anyone entering training, whether as a psychiatrist, an educational psychologist, a teacher or a social worker. Too often it makes the blood run cold.

For my part, I am truly grateful to Tom's mother for telling the story so straight, and with such moving intelligence. It is as if it were a human commentary on the 1981 Act, and the Report that went before it.

Mary Warnock

Postscript

I wrote the Foreword in 1983. Now, more than ten years on, Tom's story has come to a tragic end. What is distressing, on a more general scale, is how little we have advanced. There is still a deep reluctance on the part of professionals to have confidence in one another; and though lip service is still paid to the role of parents (and though they have increased rights to take their case to a tribunal) there is little evidence of partnership between them and the professionals. I hope now, as I did in 1983, that Tom's story will be read and taken to heart.

Mary Warnock

INTRODUCTION

This book describes the development of our son Tom, who experienced difficulties in most – but certainly not all – mental, physical and social areas. At least from the age of five he was aware of some discrepancy between his own and his peers' performances; an awareness that troubled him but which possibly also acted, for a short time, as a useful motivating force. Certainly he did increasingly well as he went through primary school, exceeding everyone's expectations for him and maybe even coming somewhere near his own ambition, to be as good as his peers – if perhaps not better than them.

When Tom was nine he began to experience bullying, partly because of his very slight hand tremor and partly because he was not as smart as his tormentors, who found several uncomplimentary names by which to advertise this fact. While some steps were taken to stop the bullying, Tom also acted to try to prove that he was not the failure he had been made to feel, for example, by attempting to amass a larger stamp collection than anyone else, though he might need to beg, borrow or steal to do so. Unfortunately, secondary school proved to be yet another bad experience as he was just not able to cope with the demands imposed upon him by so many new teachers and subjects. After a year he was transferred to a school where there was more help for children with learning difficulties but, by this time, his confidence was severely damaged, he thought of himself as a complete failure and, furthermore, the bullying continued. This time he responded by attempting to avoid, or to circumvent by one means or another, situations likely to emphasize his shortcomings; an action which tended to emphasize them more, and to invite further bullying. So he continued to withdraw and sometimes to misbehave (both at home and at school) until he was scarcely communicating, or participating, by any normal means; one particularly dramatic statement being his shoplifting, aged fifteen, of a chocolate Father Christmas.

As there had been one previous (if equally petty) offence it was decided that, this time, Tom should appear at the Magistrates Court. We, of course, attended with him and in this way came to see a report on Tom's case, written by Dr Hunt, chief psychiatrist at The Heights Psychiatric Unit for Adolescents which we had been visiting each month over Tom's fourteenth to fifteenth year. This report, having the express purpose of advising the magistrates, was certainly of great significance to us, listing as it did details from the general Case History (0-15 years). But many of those details were wrong, and others should have been invalidated by later findings; that early IQ for instance, established when he was just four years old and subsequently (at the ages of 9, 11 and 14) found to have been fifteen points too low. But it was the low score that featured prominently in the Psychiatric Report, not apparently at odds with an image of a tense, unhappy adolescent who had contributed little to meetings at The Heights, nor with parents who had, '. . . a very poor understanding of their son's limitations' (our account of his successes, years 5-9, had been received as mere fantasy). So the magistrates were advised that Tom's problems stemmed from, '. . . unrealistic demands being placed upon him both at home and at school leading to his acute sense of failure and ultimately to the shoplifting offence.' The bullying, our chief concern, was not even mentioned.

Feeling that the psychiatrist should understand how certain misunderstandings had arisen, we wrote several times requesting an interview. None of our letters was answered. Undaunted, I wrote a biography of Tom's first fifteen years. Several editors showed interest, but finally there was again rejection. Still feeling that our experience might hold useful lessons for others I looked for a new way to present the material – the result is 'Dear Psychiatrist'.

The book opens with the first letter that we wrote to the psychiatrist following the court hearing. A second letter politely asks whether the first has been received and a third (fictitious though illustrating an important point) reveals *my* growing frustration not to have received a reply. This frustration is eventually relieved with the decision to write my own version of the Case History (the clear implication being that I will send it to the psychiatrist). As this history unfolds, it soon becomes clear that my perspective is strongly influenced by our experience in court, the magistrates (conveniently upgraded to a judge and two counsels) springing into frequent focus to question my account and to throw into lively debate some of the more extraordinary aspects of it.

My purpose in writing this book is to give some idea of the enormous range of opinion and advice (from exceptionally helpful and beneficial, through negative, contradictory to even harmful) that can attend a special needs child[1] and his parents. I have also tried to show how such things as errors and prejudice which get entered into case notes can adversely affect events happening years later. However, what I most wish to do is to give some idea of the day-to-day stress that a child can feel through knowing himself to be less able than his peers, particularly if he is also the victim of ridicule and bullying. In Tom's case the loss of confidence and self-esteem that he suffered through such things checked his development far more effectively than did his handicap.

Author's Note
Pseudonyms are used throughout this book. Hospital names have also been changed.

Editor's Note
Footnotes appear on p.160.

Tom at playgroup, aged four.

7th May

Dear Psychiatrist,

The court case is now over.

 We wonder whether you are aware that reports that you write for the direction of the magistrates are handed to parents to read? We are very disturbed by many of your comments. Please would it be possible to have one more consultation to put our point of view?

21st May

Dear Psychiatrist,

We wonder whether you have received our letter of 7th May regarding your Report to the Magistrates on the case of our son Tom Roberts?

We do realize that there is much to mislead in Tom's Case History which of course you must use to compile your report; the IQ you quoted, for instance, was established when he was just four years old and later completely invalidated, being found to be fifteen points too low (test results confirming this should be in the notes at the nine, eleven and fourteen year old stages). The withdrawn uncommunicativeness so apparent when we brought Tom to The Heights Adolescent Unit aged fourteen may well have described the earlier score and hence led to some misconstructions (or what we firmly believe to be mis-constructions) regarding Tom, and also ourselves (ref. paragraph beginning, 'Mr and Mrs Roberts have a very poor understanding of their son's limitations and therefore . . .'). While we would obviously be pleased if you could modify your views, what concerns us even more is that no mention is made at all in your report of what we consider to have been the chief *nuisance* changing Tom from a happy, achieving nine year old to an anxious, uncommunicative adolescent requiring psychiatric help. *Please* could we have one more consultation to talk over these concerns?

7th June

Dear Psychiatrist,

Your silence suggests that we should be silent too . . .

. . . but nothing can stop *my* mind going back again and again to that moment in court when we were asked, 'Mr and Mrs Roberts, do you have anything that you would like to say?'

And ironically we elected to stay silent then, feeling that it would be better to bring our concerns privately to you rather than to risk the case being 'adjourned pending further investigations' for our saying something like, 'Yes, almost everything that you have just read in The Heights Report is inaccurate in some way!' But now, frustrated by the denial of that private meeting, I go on from there to explain, or to try to explain, the inaccuracies to the magistrates who have come to take on the roles of a judge and two counsels.

One *for*.

One *against*.

Dear Psychiatrist – do I need to see a psychiatrist?

I will write it all down, a Case History to set against the one that is official (that is the one, Dear Psychiatrist, that you have used in compiling your Report for the Magistrates) an undertaking in which I will be greatly assisted by the detailed notes that I have always made, both on Tom's development and also on every conversation that I ever had with a doctor, teacher, psychologist, psychiatrist or social worker about that development. I will try to be objective and to answer the questions that you might like to have answered (or even those that a prosecuting counsel might like to have answered) and to do so having regard to the truth, the whole truth and nothing but the truth.

However above all this is going to be a Case History from a parent's perspective, just one parent who would like to convey something of the ups and the downs of living with a child who does not develop in a nice steady textbook fashion, but erratically, inconsistently and to the constant delight or despair of those who worked selflessly in the hope of being most often delighted.

I will try to take account of the child's perspective too; a child who struggled to overcome one disability only to meet an intolerance perhaps more disabling. For certainly it was a key factor in turning him very gradually from an achieving, talkative nine year old to an anxious, unhappy adolescent who had virtually stopped communicating by any normal means – the 'cry for help' being a particularly pertinent example of this (I refer, of course, to the shoplifting of the chocolate Father Christmas which was to take him to court).

The history will start as the official one would, with a progress report of Tom's first year, though mine is likely to be somewhat distorted for that first year was possessed by *a scream*. A scream and a grizzly cry, the grizzly cry being my other son, Giles, one and a half years older and reacting to that scream. But I must make myself say something about that sudden high-pitched-two-o'clock-on-the-very-first-morning scream that had frozen me rigid . . .

However, my GP laughed (kindly of course) at my notion of

forceps damage. He was completely reassuring, as was my midwife – even though the *irritable cry* continued in a round-the-clock control of my nights, days, mind as I battled with hope, inadequacy, despair, exasperation and administering gripe water – which didn't soothe him. But the day that we saw the paediatrician, Dr North, at four months and one week, Tom didn't cry at all, and nothing whatsoever could be found to be wrong. So it was decided that Three Month Colic had ended a few weeks late. But it started again the next day. I'd lost what faith I'd ever had in gripe water by then – so I sang. That didn't soothe him either but it kept me sane . . .

Can we have the official line on that sanity please Mrs Roberts?

Oh that's wrong! My doctor had no worries like that, only concern, 'A week in hospital for Tom, give you a break!' – 'But the nurses couldn't walk the boards for hours on end, they'd drug him or leave him to scream. No, thank you no, I'm fine, I don't need sleep!' – 'Lucky for you! How about Bill?' – 'He's alright, he's taken up sleeping in the garden shed' – 'Oh well, no need to advise on family planning then!' I'd laughed at that so I must have been sane, but . . . 'I'm worried about Tom – he's slow' – 'Slow developer you mean! He'll catch up – by eighteen months'. No my doctor had no worries at all regarding myself or Tom. I was completely reassured. Until . . .

I remembered Giles at the same age, or met a child younger than Tom yet way, way ahead . . .

So I stuffed pillows behind his back to *make* him sit up.

My health visitor tried to be reassuring too, coming in to shake rattles behind his back and pass toys across his line of vision. But although she *said* he was doing well, I could see he didn't look round, or follow, or grasp. Besides there was the green star stuck right on the front of his notes – and this was long before green had healthy connotations. It meant (and I know because I once was a health visitor myself) *Watch this child very closely!* Which she did, banging drums behind his back and waving bright red toys across his line of vision. I'd have been so glad if he *had* taken a chocolate Father Christmas then, *anything*, though the health visitor still jollied, 'He's doing so well, will you bring him to the clinic for his birthday check? It's important as you will know, sight, hearing, vaccination – things like that to be done'.

But the clinic doctor didn't do any of those things, she just took one look at Tom and then said, very irritably, 'You needn't worry – he's not a mongol!'

But of course he's not! Such a thought was miles off . . .

Wasn't it?

It was a cold cheerless day, I remember that well, and sitting the far side of a dingy room from her, asking questions, I don't know what – only that she wasn't interested to answer. That . . . and the way she looked at Tom as if . . .

As if?

As if he wasn't worth bothering about, that's it. Not even the bother of . . . calling his name. He just wasn't worth any trouble. He did look miserable I know. He wasn't actually crying at the time, but he had cried such a lot throughout that first year that misery seemed stamped all over his face. And so we left.

It was alright though, for us, because just a few weeks later there was a complete change. The misery departed and he put on an enormous spurt.

Then he did start reaching out for red toys, green, blue and yellow ones too and, when the season was right, chocolate Father Christmases. His appetite for this last was prodigious. And not just the eating of them, the mere sight of one hanging from a tree was sufficient to trigger a quivering and squealing. He became then something of a spectacle himself, grannies, aunts, uncles, friends would sit in happy contemplation of Tom contemplating the chocolate Father Christmas. Even the clinic doctor would have been captivated by Tom aged sixteen months, perhaps you would yourself, Dear Psychiatrist, perhaps even the most dispassionate examiner . . .

Does he build four bricks? Post shapes? Climb upstairs? Oh . . .

When Tom was sixteen months old a sister, Jill, was born.

He wasn't jealous, seemed not to notice much, choosing, or continuing, to develop in his own highly individualistic way.

For instance, he sang, very early and in perfect tune all those songs that I had once sung just to keep sane. And when Tom stopped I started, wholeheartedly now, to push this skill which he came to early and did so well.

Which is to suggest that most things he did less well. And that is more or less right, though he certainly deserved advanced awards for his concoctions of baked beans, eggs and general fridge-fare, teddy bears and tea leaves, and it was quite six months before he learned all that there is to learn from stuffing the toilet with towels before flushing the cistern.

A want of discipline maybe? But when I had been so worried about lack of progress how could I possibly censure an outbreak of initiative and beans?

But is it initiative when the same exercise is repeated ad infinitum?

Oh . . . but it is normal isn't it for boys to get into mischief?

And to post shapes, build towers, constantly ask the name of!

'I'm still worried about Tom' – 'He's alright, he'll catch up!' My GP's words were just what I wanted to hear, but . . . 'He's very irritable, the slightest thing and he goes quite literally stiff with rage, do you think the forceps . . . ?' – 'Oh no, certainly not that!' – 'And after the rage he's exhausted . . .' Exhausted for hours and hours of doing nothing, hours he can't afford to waste. 'He'll catch up – by the time he's three!'

By the time he's three – that's a year to play with! And sure enough he did get to post shapes, build towers, climb stairs and, immediately after, a thatcher's ladder. That was typical of many tricks he played on us, first staggering steps at two years and two months (very late) then, just a few weeks later, right to the top. A high-climbing feat we liked to shout about (omitting, of course, to mention that the ladder had been left unguarded) whilst quietly coaxing the more basic down-to-earth skills. And the green-star-watch-this-child-very-closely people made rather less frequent checks, a school medical officer now, kind, reassuring,

'He's doing so well' – 'Yes but I am concerned, he has a high-pitched scream, do you think it could be to do with the forceps delivery?' – 'Oh no, just look at the way he's manipulating that lego! A little early yet for a comprehensive assessment, when language has developed rather more, perhaps in a year when he's three and a half'.

Three and a half, another year to play with! And a brother pulling and a sister pushing. Though usually the pull was off with his friends and the push so aggravating that Tom escaped on his own. But just occasionally things worked well, as once happened when Tom studied with his sister a mounted gavial that hangs above our stairs. 'That's a dinosaur Tom' said two-year-old Jill. 'No it's not Jill' said Tom with all the authority of his three and a quarter years, 'That's a crocodile'.

Officially that would have gone down as *strings seven words together.* Recorded in total it demonstrates the quite sophisticated level of inter-communication of which he was capable when he did occasionally connect. Another noteworthy diary entry suggests originality and a fine sense of priority, 'I like you Mum and I like ice cream'.

He liked also stripping wallpaper, (first vaulting out of his cot to do so) painting himself in creosote, staring into space for seeming h-o-u-r-s, pedalling top speed around the garden, monkey wedged in the handlebars, singing, fixing fetish-like on some fairly futile exercise and doggedly pursuing it (or, just occasionally, feverishly pursuing it), and water! At every fountain, stream or boating pool he would strip to the waist and wade in, (trousers and shoes still on) laughing, singing and frequently drawing a small crowd of amused spectators. We made little attempt to stop him for, truth to tell, we were his greatest admirers. Besides the wrath would have been terrible, to be followed by exhaustion and hours and hours of in-ac-tiv-i-ty.

If you have a child with a lot of catching up to do then every minute counts. Every minute lost will seem to widen that gap while those usefully spent will *hopefully* help him catch up, at least hold his own. Who knows? But you mustn't do anything to hinder and must do everything possible to help him towards that catch-up-by-the-time-he's-three-and-a-half-comprehensive test.

He was three and a half and a little bit more when that comprehensive test was . . . well perhaps *attempted* because today he was in a feverish-totally-consuming-squealing-at-Noddy mood and not at all interested in three identical pots. Three identical pots that could however help to decide whether you had such things as the memory, reasoning ability and motivation necessary to help you to find the red brick that you had watched being put under one of them, the three pots then being shuffled around . . .

But he could root out a kidnapped-Noddy-cum-improvised-cushion with vociferous high-pitched glee that flummoxed the doctor and put paid to the next two tests. 'Tom here's a knife, fork, spoon and – Tom look, look at this, here's a cup, Tom *look* – my goodness he's exhausting isn't he!' Yes, but strangely I'm not perturbed today, and that has something to do with the confidence born of the last time I'd expressed my fears to this particular doctor. 'Tom which do you use to stir . . . ?' For however worried I'd been in the interim period it was her total conviction that *all was well* (as he'd sat lamb-like that day, structuring lego) that I remembered. 'Tom which, *Tom* here's a cup, TOM! Perhaps you'd like to give Noddy a drink . . .'

Yes he's good at that, but it scores no marks – just fixes the next Noddy-oriented deviation that finds no use for a knife, fork, spoon just a drunk-like, rip-roaring bottoms-up, 'Tom look at this TOM! Was he a forceps?'

'Yes . . .'

And yes, and yes, and yes.

Yes he was doing well.

Yes forceps injury is what I'd suspected all along so . . . it was only a case of having my suspicions confirmed.

Yes we were lucky to have him.

Yes he was enormously attractive. Fair hair. Blue eyes. Head held slightly to one side. Appealing.

Yes it was useless to blame myself. Or anyone.

Yes there could well be other theories . . .

So it might well have been something I ate, did, didn't do.

Yes it was unhelpful pursuing that line.

Yes you are being so kind. And I can recognize that you are saying all the right things.

And one day –

I too might see things that way.

And learn to set aside guilt.

Guilt?

Oh totally irrational.

Yes I can be sure of that.

Irrational and set aside. While I try to help him forward. 'What should I be doing to help him most?' – 'Just carry on as you are, you're doing so well'.

Just carry on as you are, you're doing so well?

Well I can find a knife, fork, spoon (with nuisance-Noddy hidden deep). 'Tom which one would you use to eat your pudding? Tom! Tom which one would you use to eat ice cream? Good! And which one would you use to . . .' stab an attention slippery as melting ice! 'Tom which one, TOM which one would Mummy use to spread the butter?' Jill answers (must hide Jill tomorrow) and extends the game to a whole ward full of bandaged dolls, and Tom, 'It's ice cream and buttered bread for tea' and wonderfully imaginative stories to follow – which would so benefit Tom if only I could s-t-r-e-t-c-h that five second attention span. 'What should I be doing to most help Tom . . . doctor, paediatrician, school medical officer, educational psychologist, health visitor?' – 'Just carry on as you are, you're doing so well!'

Just carry on as you are, you're doing so well?

Yes-s-s . . .

You're doing so well?

They did say that, they really did, Dear Psychiatrist – every child specialist that I asked. I know it's ironic when viewed in the light of The Heights Report to the Magistrates, so ironic that I've found myself wondering what might have happened had I used such evidence in court, once it became clear – from reading your report – that it was *the parents* who were on trial, *the parents* (and chiefly the mother) who were seen as the guilty party, by you, and probably now by the magistrates as they filed back into court (having adjourned to consider your report) the grimmest of them then asking, 'Mr and Mrs Roberts, do you have anything that you would like to say?' And which I have always remembered as, 'Mr and Mrs Roberts, do you have anything to say for yourselves?'

"Yes," I answer fairly confidently now (having *obliged* one of the magistrates to be sure-in-my-defence, a second to take the judicial central ground, leaving only one grim-set *Mr Grey*) "I would just like to say that we were not always viewed so harshly as we have been by Dr Hunt (though I do realize that he has drawn from other professional-opinion in compiling his report). However, once upon a time, when Tom was three, four, five we, or more correctly, I, would ask every child specialist who saw Tom, 'What should I be doing to help him most?' And all of them, without exception, our GP, paediatrician, educational psychologist, school medical officer, health visitor said – though I do realize that their policy was to encourage, to reassure – but surely they wouldn't have done even that if I'd been having an *adverse* affect on Tom's development, or even one that was purely passive. For they did, every one of them say, 'Just carry on as you are, you're doing so well!'"

* * *

"Then forgive my incredulity," Mr Grey replied, his grim face stretching to describe that incredulity, "but just exactly what was it that you were doing so well?"

"Well-l-l . . ."

"Yes *well* Mrs Roberts?"

"Objection Your Honour," Mr Shore came wonderfully to the rescue, "to the blatant insult of Mrs Roberts which, furthermore, is casting aspersions on all those who were commending her."

"I do most humbly apologize," said Mr Grey with a studied bow to his Learned Friend, "such notable support cannot of course be questioned! So Mrs Roberts," he continued questioningly, "what was it that you were doing so well?"

"Oh . . ."

"Yes Mrs Roberts?"

"Tom was doing well!"

"And you were getting the praise! Never mind, perhaps we will just hear the professionals' views on Tom?"

"Oh that's difficult, but I think it's fair to say that those seeing him at a two year old level were encouraged enough to think that he might catch up by the time he was three."

"And did he?"

"No."

"I see! And after three?"

"That's not so simple, opinions varied a lot – partly because Tom himself varied . . . he was subject to many moods . . ."

"Mrs Roberts, can we please have those opinions, without editing!"

"Yes, though it might present quite a confused picture."

"I think Mrs Roberts that we can be relied upon to cope with that!" said the judge authoritatively.

"Yes-s-s, the paediatrician, Dr North, said that there was nothing much wrong but he would always be just a little bit slow. The school medical officer wasn't able to test him at all because he was so distractible, though when he was two she had found him quite normal, language delayed but hand manipulation good. The educational psychologist found his hand manipulation poor but his language good. Even so he talked about Tom as being *quite handicapped*, but not handicapped enough for special school, though he might need to be transferred to a school for slow-learning children aged seven.[2] He was hyperactive and should be put on tranquillisers otherwise the school wouldn't be able to cope. The paediatrician, at a revisit, said that on no account must he be put on tranquillisers. Playgroup said that he would make more progress if he was not so quiet and withdrawn. The school that he was due to go to, having had a report from

the educational psychologist, said that they would not be able
to cope with such a lively child unless they had a welfare
assistant[3] especially for him. The health visitor still thought him
to be doing extremely well and grannies and well-wishers
actually thought him advanced."

"Excuse me Mrs Roberts," said the judge, "I think you've
forgotten to mention your GP!"

"Oh yes, he still thought that Tom would catch up – by the
age of four and a half."

"I see, but they were all unanimous in their advice to you to
carry on as you were, you were doing so well?"

* * *

However, though the reassurances were enormously welcome,
what I had really wanted was quite specific advice on how I
might have done better. And so, in the absence of that advice, I
did *just carry on* – attempting to help forward the three year
old Tom.

Great loves – water, cats, mice, Dad – especially in his let's-
be-a-crocodile mood, sitting on Mum's knee in times of crisis,
otherwise being left to go entirely my own way.

Great hates – Jill when she's irksome, Giles when he's being
a crocodile, having to wear pants (even if Dad does), water when
it goes up my nose, and PLAYGROUP full of children like Giles
when he's being a crocodile.

Thus entry to playgroup was difficult and protracted, for even
with Mum's knee there to be stuck to, the children were still
very croc-like. And the knee was a bit slippery too, edging away,
longing to be like other knees that weren't needed. Paradoxically,
many potentially threatening situations did find him quite
fearless so that I asked myself, 'Why is it that on visits to shops,
parks and zoos my offspring explores, investigates, becomes in
fact something of a liability, yet, when it is required of him to
stand on his own two feet, he becomes so needing. Then he

looks handicapped, I feel handicapped, a failure, fed up and forced to admit *he's not ready* so give playgroup a rest for a while'.

A few months later the introduction was tried all over again, and a little more successfully for he began staying for short periods by himself. However, the day that he was furious because I had returned for him too early was followed by two weeks when he screamed at the sight of the place, refusing to be pacified. I decided that there was more to be gained from another period away from playgroup, but having instead one or two of the quieter children to play with him at home.

Determined on success I put a lot of care into this enterprise, chiefly, it seemed, for the benefit of the visiting child who invariably enjoyed himself enormously, Tom watching from the sidelines. Then, when Tom was invited to the other child's home he refused to go, or went and then screamed on the doorstep so that I again felt let down, exasperated, and that I was not doing at all well. But short of any other course or strategy I did carry on, things gradually turning around to the extent that Tom eventually came to enjoy the presence of other children, home or away. The friendships though were not founded on mutual interests, shared ideas and constant dialogue. It was more a case of Tom following where the other led and if a third child were present Tom was left out. But it was a start and by the time he was four and a half he slowly began to accept playgroup where he made friends with the supervisors, joined in some activities and occasionally played with the boys who had been to his home.

It was when he was four and a half that Tom was assessed by Mr Leroy, the educational psychologist who was to make a pronouncement on the most appropriate school placement. It was a year since the Noddy-isn't-he-exhausting test and in the lap of the gods how he would be on this day. But he seemed his much more usual quiet and quite benign self, and certainly Mr Leroy's first words upon the completion of the test (which had taken one and a quarter hours) were that he was a good little boy who did what he was told to do but soon forgot. His vocabulary was good but hand manipulation poor. I was then given the stark facts; he was quite handicapped, his IQ placing him right on the line⁴ that divides those who will go to an ordinary school and those who will need special help at a school for slow-learning children. He should start at the ordinary school at five but might need to be transferred at seven. He was hyperactive and should be put on tranquillisers.

'*Tranquillisers?*' – 'Yes, otherwise a teacher won't be able to manage him' – 'But alongside other children he's very quiet, really subdued – goes into a shell'. But Mr Leroy's heavy-duty frown seemed set to directives and deadlines . . .

Five was my deadline, he'd start school at five, half-drugged, 'And won't tranquillisers cut down brain activity, make him sluggish?' – 'Quite the contrary, they'll just cut down the hyperactivity – so he can function more normally!' . . . so he'll start school at five, drugged, and might be transferred at seven. Isn't that inevitable? Change sets him back. And what about the failure? To trail along at the bottom for two years only to be . . . 'Wouldn't it *almost* be better to start at the other school?'

That's unnatural I know, and can see from Mr Leroy's reaction. But obviously I *want* Tom to go to the ordinary school, it's just that there are worries I'm trying to sort out . . . 'He must try, it's the policy of the Department of Education to allow borderline children a two year trial'. A two year trial, so seven was the deadline in black. He's only just accepted playgroup, noise, rush, children *en masse* . . . 'And I think the best immediate policy would be a transfer to nursery school where there would be professional staff to help him' – 'But he's doing well at playgroup now and the staff are so good' – 'But not trained!' – 'And he's there with children he'll be starting school with, the nursery school's right out of the area' – 'At least go and see it and I'll write making him a priority case'.

I did go to see the nursery school but *luckily* there were so many priority cases that the supervisor said there wasn't a hope of Tom getting a place there before he was six. The paediatrician forbade the tranquillisers and, eventually (though not before it had caused all sorts of problems) the IQ was found to have been set too low. There was less talk of IQs after that, though occasional assessments were made by a new and wholly positive psychologist. Then, during The Heights Period, the old IQ was to haunt us again.

* * *

Mr Grey rose, right on cue as I realized, to a spirited defence of The Heights' taking that early IQ as accurate, "It normally remains constant does it not?" Suspicion of smug smile attends sit down, the Shore-rejoinder and the judge's pronouncement that we were, at the moment, discussing the four year old, not the fourteen year old Tom.

The four year old Tom as he emerges from a psychological test.

Which might be criticized. *How is it*, for instance, that Tom could be 'Good and obedient' in one breath and 'Hyperactive' in the next? I don't know, I've asked myself since. But not then? *How is it* that my mind so filled with the horror of that drug it was distracted from . . . DISTRACTIBILITY that's it! That's what Mr Leroy had been getting at, the job of keeping Tom's mind on course. Distractibility – is that the same as *hyper*activity? *How is it* that my mind hadn't worked as a prosecuting counsel's might to keep hold of the salient points in this review of Tom's performance in the IQ test?

So, in brief, *a good little boy who does what he's told to do but soon forgets* equals a Short Attention Span (approximately five seconds). Paradoxically it is the very attempt to direct his attention that triggers the distractibility, for left to follow his own direction and he may do so for five, six, seven, sixty seconds, sixty minutes and onwards and in a manner very far removed from hyperactivity. For he is so absorbed (or lost) as to cut out distracting influences (including, it has to be said, those that might be beneficial). So is this *control* of mind, eyes (at other times as darting as the attention) and body, that wonderful thing called concentration?

Or is it just an aspect of one of those sluggish moods that could possess him for days? The acme of which might be the snip, snip, snipping of paper with scissors and with a relentless repetition which *must* be interrupted! *Even at the risk of substituting distractibility for the perseverance?* But what value is such rigid perseverance?[5] Heaps of scrap would grow at his feet and I might try to get him to see it as snow, confetti, butterflies. And perhaps he did for a while but the butterflies continued to fall with the snow, confetti, scrap paper. So a more determined effort to lift the game – or the mood (for I know that there is just one that is good) and, all of a sudden, the room reels in a scatty tornado of snow, confetti, butterflies . . . scrap paper. *But*, just occasionally the right mood *was* struck. The paper cutting might still be done but now he talked, received, laughed, sang as he cut, saw snow scenes, weddings, Red Admirals . . .

No, that's not quite right either – just as soon as you think you've got somewhere near to describing what he was like, you then realize that you've only made a very poor stab at a hint.

And that was the problem *always* – just how to describe him. Because the way he was seen, understood, handled might be affected very much by my ability to draw a picture which adequately reflected the widely varying aspects of his temperament and abilities. Furthermore, this picture must lead to neither overestimation nor underestimation of those abilities – but rather to a constantly open mind . . .

* * *

"So we can at least take it can we Mrs Roberts that this boy was handy with a pair of scissors?"

"Oh, yes-s-s but he couldn't hold a pen, nor even the thickest of crayons – at least not sufficiently well for scribbling."

"That presumably would come with time!"

"No! Well perhaps it would, but unassisted it might have taken a very long time because there was something wrong – he apparently had a very mild form of Cerebellar Ataxia, though I wasn't told that until he was thirteen so that, at this stage, I was just bewildered."

"I don't think there's any need for the court to remain bewildered!" said the judge, deeming it best to cut through nine years of confusion.

"No – Cerebellar Ataxia is, or describes, a difficulty in performing smooth, coordinated movements so that writing was going to be enormously difficult."

"But Mrs Roberts there seems something of a paradox here! Surely smooth, coordinated movement is required for the act of cutting with scissors?" And the judge cut at the air with his fingers. And everywhere people watched, and waited for enlightenment.

"I know, I didn't understand it either! Well the physiotherapist who told me about the Cerebellar Ataxia *tried* to explain (that was when Tom was thirteen). When he was four I had no explanation at all. In fact I was quite definitely told that there was nothing physically amiss – which would have been the information that the educational psychologist was working on, possibly biasing the test."

* * *

However, neither I nor anyone else, Dear Psychiatrist, had any reason then to question the educational psychologist's findings, excepting his comments on the need for tranquillisers. Certainly he'd not even have the occasional high-elation mood at school because children *en masse* worried him. So he'd start school at five worried by children when, ideally, much learning would happen through inter-action with those children. He hardly inter-acted with the family group as yet, only joining in when it was to his advantage to do so. He rarely listened to general conversations, his attention having to be specially sought if it was necessary he should hear something. But he'd start school at five where much of the instruction would be general, *will the class please* rather than *Tom will you*. Instruction had been very specifically addressed to him during the Psychological Assessment, maybe it was even *worse* than Mr Leroy had suggested!

But he'd start school at five with a five second attention span and only just able to hold the thickest of crayons . . . unless I could do anything in the interim period to encourage the listening state, the drawn line or even the squiggle. Fortunately playgroup *eventually* saw him happier with children, making it seem that school would be that much less formidable. And Giles was a great ally, since through him we came to know the teachers, the routine, the type of things they did, said, played, the school songs, school jokes. It was also through Giles that, almost accidentally, a quite unsuspected talent in Tom was uncovered and which it seemed must be an enormous plus to take to school; and to put in the history IN UPPER CASE PRINT.

Giles, now in his third term, was struggling with the early stages of reading and not knowing anything about the look-and-say method taught at that time, I began to play I-spy type games to help him to read words phonetically. Such was Giles' difficulty that I had to sound out the whole word, add clues too to make the p-e-nny drop or the b-e-ll ring more strikingly . . . and suddenly *I* was hearing Grandsire Doubles for it was *Tom* coming up with the answers (and without his attention being specially sought). Furthermore he continued to supply the right answers, as I first checked that I was hearing right, and then developed the game in every way that I could think of; simple change through to quite sophisticated permutation. And his humour shone through, 'What does S-a-m spell?' I threw at him one day. 'Lucy' said Tom without hesitation. (Lucy was our other cat.)

That's not the sort of thing that normally gets into the notes either. But to me it was another of those noteworthy successes comparable with the early singing (and surely the two must be linked). And he learned, and very quickly, to recognize all the letters (neither did he confuse b and d). He knew the sounds made by the double consonants st, th, ch etc. and the ending *ing*

– it seemed that reading must be a whisper away.

However, though he could sound out any word that was verbally thrown at him (including the hidden n in s-a-n-d) the act of focusing his eye and attention on the written word proved so difficult that reading didn't come with any sort of facility for several years (the fact that he couldn't consolidate what he was reading by writing also delayed things). But he did start school with this very big plus . . . even if he couldn't marshall his thoughts long enough to listen to the simplest story, or his attention to take in the general class instruction. And at least he was happy to be in that class, feeling quite comfortable now with groups of children, as he was with his class teacher and welfare assistant (assigned especially to him) who were enormously kind. But impressed though they were by his purported abilities (rarely emerging spontaneously and phonetics were not done until class two) a good concentration would have been so much more helpful to them, and to him.

And to me. For, excited as I was by his many accomplishments, I would have traded them all for good concentration.

* * *

"The Neurological Stimulation Course Mrs Roberts – it is correct is it that you took your son on such a course?"

"Yes and might I say that I have rarely met such a helpful, positive and dynamic . . ."

"I haven't asked you to make a defence of the system Mrs Roberts – at least not yet!" Mr Grey added menacingly and taking a long look round as he did so. "What I, and I think the court will wish to know is whether, having embarked upon the therapy, you at least gave it a fair try before throwing it up?"

"I'm sorry, I don't understand?"

"You don't understand! Then let me read to you the relevant passage from The Heights Report, and I would just point out to everyone that this is the report that forms the main substance of the Case for the Prosecution. And I quote, 'Mr and Mrs Roberts embarked upon a course of neurological stimulation for their son but gave it up on finding it not to be effective.'"

"Oh yes, I see now. But, if I could just explain, Dr Hunt, the psychiatrist who wrote that report, hardly knew . . . well he met us just once when Tom was fifteen, so that he had to base his report mainly on what other people had said. Even so I'm not sure why he should have . . . what I *think* he's interested to do is to present Tom's history in such a way that the magistrates would be favourably disposed towards him."

"Oh come, come Mrs Roberts! Are you really suggesting that Dr Hunt has to *arrange* the material in such a way as to soften the hearts of those judging a young boy charged with the theft of a chocolate Father Christmas!"

"I object to that!" said Mr Shore jumping up, "Whether or not Dr Hunt consciously sought to effect some particular influence might be debatable. What however is quite plain, if paragraph three be read right through, is his representation of Mr and Mrs Roberts as parents who rush . . ."

"Mr Shore I think *we* are rushing things a little," said the judge. "Dr Hunt's report is largely concerned with what various professionals had to say about Tom (and of course his parents) right up to the time of his leaving school. We scarcely have him *in* school yet! Neither do we have any very useful information on the Neurological Stimulation System – excepting perhaps its potential to stir up trouble! What exactly is it?"

"Well *crawling* at the most basic level, but a highly tactile sort of crawling that it was hoped would open up new nerve routes to the brain and thus assist progress in all the other areas that were being encouraged, hand/eye coordination, language, *concentration*. But perhaps I ought just to mention that most children attending were *far* more handicapped than Tom."

"Tell me Mrs Roberts," Mr Grey then asked, "is this system more *commonly* called Doman/Delacato?"

"Yes-s-s . . . they are a physiotherapist and a neurologist respectively."

"That may well be! However if my information is correct

the system is generally frowned upon by physiotherapists *and* neurologists, in fact by the majority of the medical and educational world – is that correct?"

"Yes-s-s . . . I'm afraid so."

"So that in mentioning the physiotherapist and the neurologist you were attempting to give the system a respectability it does not enjoy?"

"Oh, I don't know – I think I was just stating facts that seemed worth stating."

"I see! And is there anything else worth stating about Doman/Delacato?"

* * *

It was completely positive, Dear Psychiatrist, that is my overriding memory. *Your child will do this.* And he would *do this* because we, at home, would steer him through the exercise regime which, we were assured, was what we needed to do to help Tom most.

Initially we'd gone to the Doman/Delacato Centre at Cheltenham just to ask questions following an article that we'd read in the *Sunday Times*. The answers we were given left us unconvinced yet wondering enough to put down Tom's name – perhaps as an antidote to that well-known syndrome 'if you don't try you'll always wonder'. However, Tom wouldn't suffer. We – or more usually *I* – would somehow contrive to do all those repetitive routines in such a way that they would be fun.

So basically mechanical exercises were turned into games; games requiring appropriate responses. And time, after time, after time it was the inappropriateness of his response which revealed to me where the real difficulties lay (chiefly in the language area).

So why hadn't I picked up those difficulties before? I don't really know – however, I have read that parents of a handicapped child will nearly always overestimate his or her abilities. Perhaps this is a type of defence mechanism against painful truth (for it is painful, *very*, to accept that your child has more serious difficulties than you had previously realized – until you also realize that, the difficulty identified, you can probably do something about it). Perhaps it is also something to do with the fact that people, quite generally, make allowances for a handicapped child to progress at a slower rate than would a normal child, but not for specific problems happening within that slowness. Tom himself was performing at a level which suggested that his comprehension was a lot more sophisticated than it actually was. In fact the official line was that there was, 'absolutely nothing wrong with his language' (language being used to include comprehension) and it was not until he was nine that one or two quite specific problems were *officially* pinpointed and remedial suggestions recommended.

However, *unofficially* (Doman/Delacato and Tom's parents) Tom was seen to have quite specific problems aged five. And once I had come to terms with the painful reality of those problems, I could also devise games to try and overcome them, aided by further ideas and – most importantly – encouragement from Doman/Delacato. In fact that was their most valuable contribution to me, their boundless encouragement and optimism together with an intense interest in Tom and a determination that he should succeed (to be honest it was almost all generated by one exceptionally talented American therapist). One day in every three months we would return to the centre to an enormous welcome and total commitment to us as every facet of Tom's progress was discussed and new goals set, together with ideas (their's as well as our own) as to how those goals might be achieved. Of course with Tom targets usually were met. However, with most children this was not the case, so that it is with some unease that I say I just wouldn't have missed the eight months that we were connected with the Centre – even though that connection was to cause us so much trouble.

* * *

"Mrs Roberts, how old was Tom when you put him on this programme?"

"Five and a quarter years."

"So that at a time when he was coping with the early stages of school he had to rush home and do these intense routines goodness knows how many times a day?"

"Well his teachers did allow him home in the afternoons to give me more time."

"Which we, no doubt, are to take as evidence of their total commitment to what you were doing?"

"*Yes*, initially they were very interested and encouraging, and as pleased as we were to have ideas on ways to improve his hand control, attention span, things like that. They even thought that they might be able to do some of the exercises at school, and then . . ."

"And then?"

"Then, right out of the blue, we got a very stiff letter from the Director of Education, pointing out our obligation to send Tom to full-time school and giving us just two weeks to comply with this regulation. A similar letter to the school was also *very* plain-speaking about Doman/Delacato, causing a change of attitudes there . . ."

* * *

It was the bitterest blow, Dear Psychiatrist, just as things were going so well. And the worst of luck because it later transpired that the Director of Education was basing his judgement very largely on another family in the county who also happened to be on the system, and who were being a considerable nuisance to him. (When we checked with Cheltenham it was to discover that this family were being a considerable nuisance to them too.) However, in response to a letter from us in which we had set down very clearly the aims of Tom's particular treatment and the one or two gains that we felt we could already ascribe to it, the Director of Education did give us permission to continue the afternoon absences, though not indefinitely. The permission was conditional on our agreeing to Tom having periodic psychological assessments to chart his progress. We gave our permission and hoped that things might now go more easily. But of course his compassionate consideration of our request did not extend to a revision of his views on the Doman/Delacato, so forcefully set out in his letter to the school as to substantially change attitudes there.

* * *

"Changed attitudes Mrs Roberts – could you be more specific?"

"Oh . . . everyone was enormously kind to Tom, I must make that clear. But I sensed a reserve . . . and I think it's fair to say there was no longer a two-way flow of ideas – that was the saddest thing, and there was considerable pressure to have him returned to school in the afternoons."

"So you returned him?"

"Oh no . . . I needed the time – I had so much to do!"

"And don't you think the school needed the time? Don't you think they had *so much to do*? Isn't it even conceivable that they may have thought that the very modest programme that they could offer was, nonetheless, rather better than Tom's crawling around in the remote chance of finding his concentration?"

"Objection Your Honour! Just because my Learned Friend has allowed himself to be persuaded by the scepticism initiated by some past Director of Education is no reason why Mrs Roberts should not be given a fair hearing now."

"I do apologize," said Mr Grey with a measured bow towards me, "though perhaps Mrs Roberts will accept that it is possible that the Director of Education alerted the school – though he may have been acting on quite faulty perceptions to have done so – to the possibility that the *crawling* routine would achieve little more than advanced crawling."

And Mr Grey's eyes coursed the court to encourage the laugh so that it would again be difficult to persuade anyone that it might have been otherwise, even though I could this time describe a progression to writing, first wild scribble to complete words.

"And by *freehand* you simply mean *unrestrained by lines* do you Mrs Roberts?" Mr Grey interrupted my account.

"Initially I mean, quite literally, *freely* with his hands."

"Using finger paints?"

"Yes – but sand on the floor was much better!"

"You live in a cave do you Mrs Roberts?"

"Mr Grey, I imagine that Mrs Roberts would put down a sand tray," said the judge, extending the humour with very evident enjoyment.

But the reality had actually been more cave-like, with a bucket of sand thrown on the floor and Tom crawling through it, laughing and singing and drawing with his fingers as he went.

"Ah – so we did achieve advanced crawling!"

"I object to the *we* achieved," said Mr Shore acidly, "for I hardly think that my Learned Friend will be thought to have contributed very greatly to this advance!"

But Mr Grey still glowed with the satisfaction of his own advanced line.

* * *

And that, Dear Psychiatrist, as I am sure you will know, represents fairly accurately the prevailing professional-scepticism regarding all things Doman/Delacato. And nothing that I have said thus far will alter it; the writing, after all, happened only as an indirect consequence of the crawling. However, and be that as it may, the crawling was a vital vehicle to writing for once he had realized, from his hands-and-knees artistry, what good fun drawing could be, he became sufficiently motivated to put in whatever extra effort was required towards full pen-handling (previously he had been totally uninterested in any type of drawing activity). From sand he progressed to chalks, still on the floor, scribbling at first, then pictures of people, trees, animals of every shape and size . . . and letters, shaky, dishevelled, back-to-front, upside down, right hand, left hand – they came right in the end. And he was writing on paper now with thick pens, not neatly of course but forming recognizable letters. I cut up paper sacks to give him plenty of room and to satisfy his insistent demands for *more paper*. Of course he could read a little and had known all his letters before going to school so that now he had this new ability, and once he felt really ready (by his sixth year), he launched straight into sentences . . .

* * *

"*Koala wants his medicine* was the first thing he ever wrote, I'll never forget it!"

"So you returned him to full-time school?"

"I object to that Your Honour! My Learned Friend's contributions would seem to be rather less imaginative than the young Tom's!"

"What exactly are you saying Mr Shore?"

"Pressed to an explanation I'd say that he, that is my Learned Friend, is becoming every bit as predictable as a school bell!"

"Which must be answered!" said the judge, looking at me.

"Oh yes, yes there was pressure to have Tom returned . . . but I pleaded more time, because I was working on language now . . ."

* * *

And then, Dear Psychiatrist, it was discovered, quite by chance, that the Director of Education had never sent a letter to the Head Master informing him of the changed ruling on the afternoon absences, so that for three months or so the school had thought that I'd been taking Tom home at midday in an openly defiant gesture. I was able to show the Head Master the letter that we had received, a copy was taken and I again had reason to hope that things would go better. But the pressure to return Tom to afternoon school continued.

There was another pressure too, Dear Psychiatrist, regarding that *possible transfer to Special School at seven.* For although Tom was making these great strides, his concentration was non-existent (or programmed to his private world), so that he was always trailing in comprehension, out on a limb, the odd one out. Furthermore the Head Master kept on referring to that *possible transfer* and in a way that seemed it was not so much a possibility as already decided . . . 'Do you think it's likely?' – 'Quite honestly Mrs Roberts I can't see him making it at my school!' . . . but he can write, and quite unaided, though I dare not say so for conditions have to be so perfect that he would never give a demonstration, although perhaps next term when he moves to class two where phonics is used . . . 'And he must stay in this class another term!' – 'Oh but he's set his heart on moving up, particularly as Jill will be in this class – he's determined to stay ahead' – 'He must stay here!' He was *here* where we spoke, arranging Jill's admission. Here, yet not here, divorced as he seemed from everything going on all around. His teacher (who did recognize that he'd made great strides) was chiefly concerned that he did not *move with the class*, so that she must say, 'Will the class put their books away,' followed by, 'Tom will you . . .' And it seemed chiefly for this reason that he couldn't move with the class to the next class.

Tom was very upset about this, knowing that he was a lot better than Aran and Lance who were moving. For on a basic *what was unfair* or *uncomfortable* level he was very switched-on indeed. He didn't like children's parties because, 'I never do well in the games Mum'. He didn't like the attentions of a special helper because it made him feel *different*. Besides, 'Aran and Lance don't have one and they aren't so good as what I am'. And he didn't like the specially packaged, 'Tom get your books!' – which would keep happening unless he could develop a constant listening state. That's what was missing, a *constant listening state*. Sometimes he seemed as isolated as a deaf child in the remoteness of his private world.

But I had made a discovery, several linked discoveries, that I was absolutely sure was the way to this listening state, if it was possible at all, and that was through language, very specially monitored language.

But I needed the time, the quiet afternoon time . . .

* * *

"And did the Director of Education approve of your keeping Tom away from afternoon school in order to do this language work?"

"I object Your Honour! A mother does not normally need approval to teach the Mother Tongue."

"In school hours she may well do!" said the judge. "So Mrs Roberts, please tell the court precisely what this language work entailed."

Which was difficult in an atmosphere of such evident scepticism and in the presence of undisputed Masters of The Word. Would, "Talking as we played with whatever interested him" pass? "Sand, water . . ."

"At least water would be very therapeutic!" said Mr Grey like an icy repeat of that self-same cold water. He complained too that there didn't seem to be much wrong with Tom's language, "In fact Mrs Roberts, don't I remember your saying that the educational psychologist, or was it the school medical officer, considered Tom's language to be good?"

"Yes – the educational psychologist . . . and his teacher."

"Yes! You see Mrs Roberts, when you report such things,

and when you further report his first written words to be 'Koala wants his medicine' then it does not seem that there can be very much wrong with this child's language!"

"Yes, I know . . . but if I had said, 'Koala's medicine is in the fridge' he wouldn't have known where to look for it."

"Oh come, come Mrs Roberts, this child who has been removing eggs from the fridge with impunity, and from the age of two years?"

"Well . . . most of the time I had the fridge tied up with string so he couldn't get in! Even so, no, I couldn't believe it either. But eventually, after about six rephrasings of my question, I had to. I didn't want to, I was very worried, it seemed to me perhaps the first sign of what might turn out to be a very complex problem."

"Which you are no doubt shortly going to try to convince us it turned out to be. However, let us stay for one moment with the simple fact – for I imagine we must take it as simple fact – of your son's failure to know what or where the fridge was. Such ignorance it seems might have been picked up before – by Koala if not by yourself!"

Only Mr Shore held loyally aloof from the laugh. And the portraits of three past dignitaries that hung above the judge remained too, loftily composed. I had been appalled yes, at my failure, at Tom's lack, and at great pains to find the explanation for myself then, and for Mr Grey now. "So how are we to understand," he said when I had finished, "that Tom had first been shown the fridge?"

"Maybe he was shown the egg," threw in the judge and raising a hand in the air, cupped to the exact shape of his idea.

"Fridge or egg, egg or fridge," mused Mr Grey, "or perhaps Mrs Roberts your instructions to Tom were just not exciting enough! Maybe if you had said, 'Take an egg from the fridge and break it' he would have been happier to oblige!"

"I object to that Your Honour! My *Learned* Friend has quite obviously failed to appreciate that for Tom to have followed this instruction correctly would merely have indicated that he knew what and where the *egg* was and, arguably, that he had some understanding of the concepts *get* and *break it* – though of course in the second instance an accident of chance may have intervened. Furthermore, if this much be understood, it is also quite apparent that it cannot be assumed that Tom either listened to *or* analysed the original instruction correctly."

"Or maybe it was that Mrs Roberts had the fridge tied up with string so that Tom couldn't get in and the egg couldn't get out!" said Mr Grey in a type of fridge and egg logic owing something to the length of the string. (And he actually held out his hands in a no-string-so-we'll-never-know despairing gesture. And sat down.)

But I was given more time.

"And the burning question," said Mr Grey jumping up again, "did he learn where the fridge was?"

"Oh . . . I hope so, inadvertently, it was mostly a case of . . . we mainly talked about flowers."

"*Flowers?*" said Mr Grey, his hands again shooting out to empty despair and his brow up to astonished interrogative.

"Yes-s-s . . . it was his great passion of the moment."

"*Great passion?*"

"Mr Grey," interrupted the judge, "I hardly think that this is the type of Great Passion that the court will wish to spend undue time upon. What we really have to decide is whether Mrs Roberts was, at this stage, an adverse influence upon her son's development (that being, of course, the main thrust of The Heights Report). If she was merely talking about flowers . . ." Here the judge took a look around the court, a broad benevolence in his smile, "surely it would have been completely harm- less . . . surely!"

* * *

Dear Psychiatrist,
I was reading a lot of books at this time on the development of language. And though my fascination might in part have been

an expression of that other well-known syndrome 'everything in the textbook fits my case', a great deal of what I read did at least seem relevant and, at times, breathtaking, *Attention develops from the acquisition of language.*[6] And in the same book, *An artificially hastened acquisition of speech may lead not only to enrichment of speech activity but also to substantial reorganization of the child's whole mental development.* Conversely, *Poor speech development will lead to retardation of all the intellectual processes connected with speech, in particular the processes of abstraction and generalization.*

Though I can no longer find its source, one textbook-line has lodged in my mind for its being so applicable to Tom, *Rigid thought patterns leading to stylized and ritualistic play.* In practice this meant, for instance, that he might push a toy car round and round a track and never think to deviate from this course (the paper-snipping described earlier might serve as another example). And the rigid thought patterns were very evident in his speech where he might ask the same question over and over again without really pausing to hear the answer. Asked a question himself and he would frequently snatch at some readily available answer that was usually inadequate in some way. However, having decided upon it he could not easily be persuaded to move on to one that was better. Most unbending of all was his *ruling* on words with two meanings, for example *light* he would accept as light from the sun but absolutely refuse in a weight context. In arithmetic his teacher reported that he understood 3+3=6 but adamantly rejected any other combination that will also make six.

I didn't really know what to do about all this but obviously to talk about his 'passion of the moment' offered the best chance of the first essential – *to hold attention.* That the subject matter should be capable of various interest also seemed desirable and here I was to find flowers a wonderfully fertile field.

For a start they were so abundant (and by good fortune it happened to be springtime when this interest was beginning). They were delightful to look at, smell and sometimes to pick, their sheer variety alone seeming to defy any fixed notions. It was, however, the wealth of ideas embodied in such names as King Cups, Foxgloves, Dandelions and Forget-me-nots that was to prove so particularly useful.

I told him why Elephants Ears, Cranes Bills and Snap Dragons had come by their names, but initially he could not extend the idea to tell me why Birds Eye might have been so-called. Soon, however, he was not only making this type of connection himself, he was also beating me at my own game, for after I had told him how Day Lilies and Jack-go-to-bed-at-noon had acquired their names he asked me if Evening Primroses lasted one night. There were flowers named after their spreading potential, Creeping Jenny, Mile-a-minute, Runner Beans, Jack-around-the-hedge (otherwise Convolvulus, and that one has about ten rampant names), whilst Feverfew and Woundwort advertised medical properties (Tom freely improvised on this theme, renaming the sting-relieving Dock Leaf a *Doctor* Leaf). Some flowers, such as House Leeks, were embedded in folklore; others, like the Passion Flower, had stories woven around their structure. Flowers could be cut, pressed, arranged, in vases – or in any other group that took our fancy, those that were red, those that lived in the water, began with T, opened in spring, had an animal in their name – the possibilities were endless.

Tom studied them, picked them, talked about them, morning, noon and night. He could always be guaranteed to join in wholeheartedly with whatever flower foray was on offer. However, there was one problem in that his enthusiasm was such that it frequently tripped the repetitive-questioning ritual, tending in turn, to trigger some flower fixation.

Be that as it may, in the realm of flowers Tom's thoughts took on a new dimension. He was for instance bad at linking one piece of information with another to arrive at a new idea, but said to his father, 'Picking all the flowers is like taking all the birds' eggs' for he had linked Bill's explanation of the cycle of plant life to an earlier talk on the purpose of eggs. He was poor at ordering events in their correct time sequence yet quite spontaneously described a flower maturation process, 'First it's a tight bud, then it's fully out and then it's sorry for itself'. He was bad at listening to a long question and holding its various parts in mind whilst scanning his memory for the necessary information, yet a question starting, 'Can you think of a flower which is . . . ?' followed by two to three clues to the required answer, posed no problems for him. He was not very good at using his knowledge in order to predict what might be the result of a certain action, but volunteered, 'That Periwinkle is going to escape from Mr Smith's garden into Mrs Weaver's garden, they will have to share it'. He could even cope with such abstract subtleties as appear in riddles, so long as they had a flower connection.

The main thing that I did in attempting to address the rigid thought tendancy was to use words in unusual contexts. Tom was fascinated by this and quickly became very experimental himself. 'Is that a *patch* of ducks over there?', 'This dumpling's very lazy' (as it stuck persistently to his fork), 'My hair's spilling over my shoulders to meet my back', 'Why is Dad shaving the greenhouse?' He tried to describe a sensation, 'The ginger beer went up my nose' and when he spilt some thought it might sting his toes.

Impressive though all this was, it seemed that such versatility of thought was reserved mainly for high-interest flowers. This was tantalizing because I knew he *could* receive and transmit adequately, but so much of the time he was stuck on one of his poor quality programmes where he would be for ever destined to miss out, be the odd one out, sit by himself. *Pay attention Tom.*

And he was already, aged six, devising quite clever avoidance tactics, especially when the speaker happened to be his sister. 'Wasn't that a lovely story – shall I tell it again?' Jill asked at the completion of a somewhat wordy tale that she had somehow contrived from the Oxford English Dictionary. 'No!' said Tom, very firmly, 'Because Koala and me are just going to start our winter sleep.' – 'Well I think I will anyway,' said Jill just as firmly, 'because Lamb Chop, Frogbit and Chicken weren't listening, *and neither were you Tom*, are you ready? Once upon a time . . .'

. . . there was a boy who this time fell off his seat because Koala had pinched him. Brought to heel (or back to his seat) he did hear the pay-attention-beginning, as he usually did in the end, wherever he was, because it was an order. But having stayed for this he could hibernate, or busy himself with his own thoughts (so long as they didn't involve falling off chairs). Sometimes he was so busy with his own thoughts that he landed up right in the middle of a pay-attention-sum (having completely missed the happily-ever-after ending). And there were pay-attention-spellings and pay-attention-games and even a pay-attention-lady and a pay-attention-table – just for him. He hated the pay-attention-table-just-for-him. But to move to the ordinary-table-like-everyone-else he had got to move with the once-upon-a-time beginning, through the this-and-that-middle, to the happily-ever-after-ending with everyone else . . .

'. . . and that's the end. Wasn't that a lovely story! Shall I tell it again Tom? *Tom* shall I tell it again? TOM!'

* * *

"MRS ROBERTS! I was asking – how old was Tom when he began full-time school?"

"Oh . . . six years."

"I see, so that aged six he became a completely normal member of school?"

"In that he attended nine to three o'clock, certainly. It was the fact that he didn't attend . . . sorry, I was trying to give some idea how things were aged six to seven, which in many ways was quite staggering . . ."

"*Staggering!*" said Mr Grey with an appalled intonation that exclaimed around the court. "Perhaps," he continued, and drawing thumbs and fingers down each of the linen bands that fell from his neck, "it would be of most help to have Tom described as his teachers might have seen him". And he gave a little tug on the bands which he still gripped at the ends.

"Oh yes he had two teachers over this period, plus his special helper." That was the easy bit, but how to go on . . . ? "He was the subject of enormous goodwill, that was the most important thing to me, the thing most likely to make him succeed." What *was* succeed . . . to stay put – to move to the table with everyone else . . . *personally I can't see him making it at my school* . . . a tug on the bands . . . pay attention!

"*Succeed* Mrs Roberts, I'd have thought . . ."

"At *that* school, and that meant moving with everyone else . . . beating the distractibility. The Head Master was convinced a Special . . ."

One linen band fell free as Mr Grey leaned forward to write DISTRACTIBILITY. What about ACHIEVEMENTS! The reading, writing, language, ideas . . . 'Couldn't he *try* sitting at a table with other children?' – 'It wouldn't work, he wouldn't work then everyone would suffer (and don't forget Jill will be one of them) then I'll quite definitely have to recommend Special . . .' PAY ATTENTION!

"Sorry, I've forgotten what I was saying . . ."

"The Head Master's views Mrs Roberts – on your son!"

"Oh yes, he strongly felt that a Special School would be best, right up to within three months of Tom being seven. By then a school for slow learners seemed quite ludicrous – but to have the threat lifted was wonderful . . ." ('Just because ESN is no longer appropriate doesn't mean that things are normal Mrs Roberts, they're a long way from that and I wouldn't want you to run away with the wrong idea . . .') "Though almost immediately he – the Head Master – started talking about a school for the physically handicapped, but not until Tom was eight."

"Mrs Roberts forgive me if I'm being slow," said the judge, leaning forward with stern attention, "but when you talked about Tom *moving with the class* I understood you to mean in a mental sense, keeping his mind . . ."

"I did! There *was* a coordination problem but hardly . . . well I suppose it just didn't seem a big problem to me because I could only think HE'S WRITING NOW . . . but, incredible as that seemed, I'd have traded the writing *and* the reading for a good concentration!"

"*Concentration* – isn't that why you started with the Doman/Delacato?" said Mr Grey, tugging twice on his bands, to the *man* and the *cato*.

"Oh, one of the reasons yes, and yes, we did finish there without achieving concentration . . . but they'd given us all sorts of ideas that had generated others . . ." . . . words, words, words – just playing around with words. Words were the key, or seemed to be: *Attention develops from the acquisition of language.* But supposing there are fundamental problems with reception, analysing, recall – will structured language training help then? *Carefully modulated speech training may lead not only to enrichment of speech activity but also to substantial reorganization of the child's whole mental development* . . . but results are so erratic, sometimes mental agility is astounding, at others . . . *Parents generally seem to be quite naive regarding their child's ability to process language – clinicians might best serve the child's development by* . . . Just carry on!

"Your concentration seems to have lapsed Mrs Roberts!"

"Oh, sorry . . ." The concentration was now intense around the court as everyone waited. "We took him to see Dr Heckman of the Fairlands Psychiatric Unit for Young Children."

"*A Psychiatrist!* For this child whose main problem – at least as far as the Head Master is concerned – would seem to be physical?"

"He *was* concerned about the concentration, distractibility, things like that – and Dr Heckman was a leading figure in these matters, we *had* to go.

* * *

Dear Psychiatrist,

I don't suppose you will need any explanation as to why we chose to see a psychiatrist at this stage (Tom was six). However, since our route was unconventional, I should perhaps describe it.

I had at this time a Canadian friend who was living locally

whilst writing a dissertation on *The Importance of Language in Education* for her Master's Degree. She, not unnaturally, was fascinated by Tom. She was also a fount of useful information on every aspect of language/perceptual development. Recognizing my interest in the subject, she invited me along to the inaugural lecture of her Professor of Psychology; a lecture which touched at some point on concentration which, we were told, *developed along well-recognized pathways.* Thinking that an understanding of these pathways might inform very usefully the type of work I was attempting, I wrote to the professor, briefly stating my interest and asking if he could give me any further information or point me towards helpful literature. He wrote back saying, 'I think the best thing that I can do is suggest a really able and professional man who might advise you. He is my colleague, Dr Jeremy Heckman of the Fairlands Psychiatric Unit for Young Children, who is renowned for his work, particularly with children who have concentration and distraction problems'. With this much encouragement I wrote to Dr Heckman receiving, some time later, a reply. Although I had again only asked to be *pointed towards helpful literature,* Dr Heckman was suggesting that he actually saw Tom, and both parents. However, we must first get a letter of referral from our GP as Fairlands was a National Health Institution. The letter suggested that the investigations would take a long time. Furthermore, repeated assessment would be necessary if adequate education and advice were to be arranged.

So not only were we to be given advice, but Tom was to have his education monitored by specialists in this field. We were delighted; but a little upset that it had been necessary to find this advisory expertise for ourselves.

* * *

"So Mrs Roberts," said Mr Grey, bouncing back into perspective, "a great deal was invested in this visit!"

"Yes!" A bit like asking for the sky – and hope had soared with that welcoming handshake. "I had to wait while Dr Heckman read through Tom's notes, making comments as he did so; comments that were arresting, unorthodox, irreverent, generating in me a sort of exhilaration – we were not going to be sent away with bland statements, mere platitudes . . ."

"By which I take it you mean that you were not going to be told, *Carry on as you are, you're doing so well!*"

"No! Far from it – but that's a long way off."

"And we are absolutely bound are we," said Mr Grey with pained emphasis as he looked all around, "to experience every nuance of mood and emotion on the way to this far-off opinion?"

"Oh I was trying . . ." What was I trying . . . ? To recreate the dynamics? Give some idea of expectations . . . set-up, or imagined? "Since this consultation is with a *psychiatrist*," the Judge interrupted my uncertainty with a decision worthy of Dr Heckman himself, "and since a Psychiatric Report lies at the very heart of the case, I feel that Mrs Roberts should, in this instance, report as fully as she feels fitting – though perhaps you could concentrate on what was actually said!" he added more directly to me.

"Yes, from his reading of the notes Dr Heckman had gained the impression that Tom's problem was chiefly physical and a little bit educational. I told him that I would definitely put the educational problem first and began to explain about the poor concentration and certain difficulties to do with abstract thought, whereupon he became quite alarmed and remonstrated, 'Oh my goodness you mean he's got *that* problem and nothing's been done? We must act quickly'." So I wasn't asking for the sky! Why hadn't we come here before? Why hadn't we been sent? "And without further delay he began taking the Case History from me, frequently interrupting in the interests of greater accuracy, the fuller picture. He . . . thought we were mad to have tried the Doman/Delacato, but I had to be fair and told him how good the therapists had been, 'Humph, we see the results, exhausted, disillusioned parents and children who are nervous wrecks' but . . ."

"Stop there Mrs Roberts!" And Mr Grey put up his hand policeman-like and wrote with the other, "The parents became exhausted through doing the programme?"

"So he said though obviously . . ." *obviously* I am suspect unless I can show myself capable of a calm, clear judgement which can distinguish between the repetitive, stereotyped exercises, and those – which we concentrated upon – to promote such things as listening, anticipation, reasoning . . . the restraining hand again, as Mr Grey seemed to record every word in his notes, whilst Dr Heckman had remained contemptuously dismissive – stupid to be offended, all part of his outrageous personality which would step on anyone and anything to GET THINGS DONE.

"'Haven't you had his eyes tested?' Dr Heckman threw at me as I was *trying* to impress upon him that the therapists were the first people to recognize (and treat) a hand/eye coordination problem. 'Oh my goodness gracious me,' he went on, 'here we have a child of school age and absolutely nothing's been done'." (So something could be done, he'd said it again!) "Then on we raced, delving into every aspect of Tom's developmental history (prenatal to the present) which frequently I could not give in sufficient detail, 'That tells me nothing – I'll have to get the notes from your doctor!' he admonished. He was equally critical of some of the comments made by professionals in the Case History, particularly Mr Leroy's diagnosis of hyperactivity – though he took very seriously things that I said about the poor concentration and a whole range of associated difficulties in reasoning, recording, recall and so on. And I asked specific questions about games that I played in attempting to address these problems. 'What do you do with your spare time?' he answered. 'I don't have any, I spend it all working with Tom,' I replied, still waiting for the advice that might make that work – or play – more effective. 'Then stop doing anything!' he ordered before rushing on to list work *he* wished to have done; a skull X ray, a psychological reassessment, genetic and eye tests, EEG.[7] He was very apologetic about putting Tom through so many procedures and for the nuisance it would all cause, but stressed that the tests were very necessary – then he told me it was all my fault that they hadn't been done already. It was absurd." Wasn't it? Yes of course I asked why . . . "'Because you're so overprotective you haven't allowed them to be done!'" And down went OVERPROTECTIVE. "Of course it *must* have been a joke, I wasn't . . ." The restraining hand was raised again and OVERPROTECTIVE stayed. "Did Dr Heckman test Tom at all that day?" Mr Grey asked, lowering his hand, a suspicion of a smirk serving to suggest, *if of course you allowed it!*

"Only a tearing-up-paper test to assess his willingness to stick at *the most boring job in the world* – he passed with distinction!"

"Meaning he would have stuck at it till Kingdom Come?"

"Yes."

"So was this a test of his concentration?"

"Oh no, it was purely a test to prove the psychologist wrong in using the term *hyperactive* to describe Tom."

"Which the test did?"

"Yes – I think however there was a difference of definition here, Mr Leroy probably used *hyperactive* in the sense of a child whose mind couldn't keep on course, whereas I happen to know that before Dr Heckman will use that term a child would probably have to be eating the paper as he climbed up the wall as well."

"I see, so he wasn't hyperactive, but there was no argument regarding the poor concentration?"

"None at all! That's what pleased me – everything I said triggered this dramatic response, 'Oh my goodness you mean he's got *that* problem and absolutely nothing's been done! We must act quickly, this is most urgent!'"

"And did you have no qualms about all this testing that was proposed?"

"Objection Your Honour! Mrs Roberts cannot first be accused of not allowing tests to be done and then of allowing them!"

"Apparently she can Mr Shore. Please continue Mrs Roberts."

"No I didn't have any qualms because Dr Heckman made it quite clear that he needed the precise information that the tests would give in order to advise on the most appropriate treatment. And neither did my husband object – he'd also been called in towards the end of the consultation to have the tests explained. We both said that we were absolutely delighted that someone was taking so much interest. Dr Heckman then apologized that he wouldn't be making the recommendations personally once the tests were completed, as he was just off to Australia for six months – but he would ask a colleague to take over the case. We were very sorry I remember, feeling it unlikely that anyone else would match his vitality and determination to get things done. But, we had miscalculated very badly there, because Dr Heckman forgot to order the tests so that by the time . . ."

"Mrs Roberts I find that very hard to credit – that Dr Heckman should forget to order them!"

"Well all, that is, except the psychological reassessment."

"Then please be more accurate!"

"Objection Your Honour! Is that all the comment that my Learned Friend is prepared to make? Does he not see that this is precisely the type of careless oversight that might drive a patient to the alternative services? And by *alternative* services I am thinking in particular of Doman/Delacato," Mr Shore added with a meaningful look at his Learned Friend. "Or are we maybe to think," he continued, his eyes now sweeping the court, "that the oversight was in fact quite deliberate, either because Dr Heckman felt that Mrs Roberts was so overprotective she wouldn't allow the tests to be done, or perhaps that Tom was too much of a nervous wreck to have them done!"

"Mr Shore I would ask you not to be so frivolous," said the judge sternly, "presumably Dr Heckman forgot such things in his rush to get to Australia. Please continue Mr Grey."

"Thank you Your Honour. You were able to get the tests done were you Mrs Roberts?"

"Yes, but it was extremely difficult as Dr Heckman had left no indication in the notes that he wished them to be done, so getting the tests authorized proved very difficult."

"But since you did get the tests authorized and done you report the whole thing as a totally negative piece of information."

"I object to that Your Honour! Is it not significant that Mrs Roberts might have earned for herself a label of *anxious parent* in having to worry others for these tests? Might she not actually have become anxious – even a *nervous wreck* at the inevitable delays, given that she had been led to understand that the case was urgent?"

"Mr Shore I would remind you that it was the boy who risked becoming a nervous wreck, the mother merely *exhausted and disillusioned.*"

* * *

But the disillusionment, perhaps *let down* would be better, happened very gradually Dear Psychiatrist, because I made myself wait two or three weeks before making the enquiries which eventually led to the disclosure that the tests had not been ordered.

Excepting the psychological reassessment which was quickly arranged and kindly conducted by Mr Strickland, the senior psychologist to the Fairlands Unit. I was invited to stay to what eventually turned out to be an extremely interesting afternoon, though initially Mr Strickland seemed very unsure about what to do, leading me to think he'd perhaps had some unusual request from Dr Heckman. He even resorted to asking Tom what he'd done with Mr Leroy last time, but when Tom (who'd been four that last time) said, 'We played in the garden' Mr Strickland did decide on a more conventional line of testing. Questions first to fix his awareness level and which produced some vintage Tom. He did well too on the reading, simple jigsaws and tests with bricks; 'Put seven of those bricks in a box' – correct – 'Put them all in the box except three' – correct – 'Repeat these numbers' – correct up to five digits – 'Reverse these numbers' – correct – 'Can you make the patterns on your bricks match this shape?' – yes if it's a straightforward circle or square – and on to a code, good to begin with, then gets agitated and makes mistakes. All helping to build up picture.

But it was a black box which brought to light the most significant finding. I had read all about this box in a book by the psychologist A.R. Luria and its value in revealing language and perceptual problems. The box consisted of two screens, either of which Mr Strickland could light by a green or a red light. Tom could extinguish these lights by pulling on the appropriate cord, one of which hung down from each side. Tom's first instruction was to extinguish the green light only, it appearing initially only on the right side, and then at random, either side. Tom coped with this well. The next stage was for Tom to say 'Now' when the green light appeared. This was also done satisfactorily. Tom then had to combine both responses, saying 'Pull' as he pulled the cord to the green light. Here he got hopelessly confused.

I was confused too, the spoken word was supposed to facilitate the manual task and I waited for Mr Strickland to enlighten. However, he wanted me to tell him what I had noticed and was so insistent that I eventually did, in the context of what I'd read *should be* and what obviously *wasn't*. 'Exactly, that's the problem!' said Mr Strickland, seemingly delighted by this mutual starting point – or by the significance of the finding. And he went on to explain that Tom's motor and speech systems were not properly coordinated. He explained too that the systems do, quite normally, develop separately, becoming integrated later – and then he went on beyond the mutual understanding to some very cerebral theory. Though certainly his excitement was quite evident, and contagious, for surely now that the problem had been identified there must be ways to . . . 'Is there something I can do, some game I can play to help the coordination to happen?' Mr Strickland looked surprised, and then went on talking about things which didn't seem connected with ways I might help. 'Would puppets be useful? There he'd be accompanying the spoken word with hand movements?' Mr Strickland continued to talk at length and in depth . . . but without actually mentioning puppets, which I'd long found useful allies in language/*perceptual* training. This might also sound cerebral, but in fact was just a case of Koala being one step behind the audience in solving some down-to-earth problem, the audience, of course, being Tom.

So Tom became the puppeteer – though without any significant improvement. Perhaps there was nothing that could be artificially done. And soon we became engaged in day-to-day happenings, the black box findings just a good memory of a significant afternoon.

That is until we met Dr Heckman again, six months after our first consultation, for advice following the completion of the tests. Once again there was the wait while he read through the notes, and once again it was the comments he uttered whilst doing so that set the mood – very different today, almost too casual, for Tom's problems seemed far more complex than could be adequately explained by the easy assurances we were catching . . . or by one simple diagnosis following on the black box disclosures, 'You don't know about that Mr Roberts? Obviously your wife doesn't talk to you! It is a valuable piece of equipment which . . .' . . . your wife in fact described quite fully to you five months ago as being very useful in disclosing language/motor coordination problems – problems that Tom has, amongst others.

* * *

"Are you going to keep the court in suspense Mrs Roberts? Or are we to hear what Dr Heckman advised?"

"Yes, Dr Heckman gave us a diagnosis of Benign Cerebella Dysphasia which he explained was a long-sounding name to describe a failure of the speech and motor systems to become completely integrated. He then added that Tom could expect to be free of the condition by the time he was seven."

"You didn't believe him did you Mrs Roberts?" said Mr Grey, his piercing eyes seeming to stare straight through me.

"Oh . . . no, it's funny – I didn't say so of course, but I did find it hard to believe that Tom would just grow out of his problems."

"I don't think it funny at all Mrs Roberts. Any doctor will

tell you that 90% of the cure is trust and belief in the doctor."

"But . . ."

"How old was Tom at this time?"

"Six years and eleven months."

"And was Dr Heckman aware of Tom's exact age when he gave you that very precise prediction?"

"Yes, because he checked the age in the notes. And when he realized there were but four weeks to go he asked me if I had noticed any changes already."

"And you no doubt said that you had not noticed anything dramatic!"

"Yes – they were almost my exact words."

"But Dr Heckman remained certain in spite of your negativity?"

"Yes."

"Then he must have been very sure of himself mustn't he Mrs Roberts?"

"Yes he was."

"And was anything else to happen? Did he advise any treatment?"

"Yes, he said that two terms of good remedial teaching would effect the cure and that he would speak to the Director of Education on the matter."

"Ah, so is it a spontaneous or an aided recovery that we are talking about?"

"I don't really know – I imagine it was hoped that the two would go hand in hand."

"Plus that other vital ingredient of the mother's – perhaps we should say, the parents' – believing that the recovery would take place!" said Mr Grey, the eyes still piercing.

"Yes I suppose so – but Tom never got the remedial teaching."

"One moment Mrs Roberts," interrupted the judge, "I thought that Tom had a special helper, a welfare assistant all to himself?"

"Oh yes, but she had no teaching qualifications. She was really an extra pair of hands for the class teacher. A very good pair of hands but . . ."

"Not a qualified teacher!"

"No, and of course it was someone with expertise in teaching children with learning problems who was needed – for two terms. Dr Heckman was quite specific regarding the length of time."

"Well, knowing the way things go, two terms would have passed before anything could be set up," said the judge, sitting back in his chair and indicating with a nod that Mr Grey should resume the questioning.

"So it's really your negative attitude to be dealt with," said Mr Grey resuming, "Did Dr Heckman give you any advice to encourage a more positive outlook?"

"He certainly told us to forget every single thing that the educational psychologist had ever told us, particularly the IQ. But of course not everything was as suspect as that, the tranquillisers and the hyperactivity issue – and Mr Leroy was still officially monitoring Tom's . . ."

"You went there seeking Dr Heckman's advice and then refused to take it!"

"Oh I didn't challenge him over anything – I kept my feelings strictly to myself."

"He was a psychiatrist Mrs Roberts – he could no doubt read your mind. You needed it seeing to for taking Tom to that crackpot Delacato place for a start!"

"But they were so helpful they . . ."

"THE RESULTS MRS ROBERTS – EXHAUSTED PARENTS AND NERVOUS WRECKS OF CHILDREN!"

"Mr Grey do you have to shout?" shouted the judge, "Mrs Roberts gave no hint that she herself was exhausted by the course which she furthermore *insisted* that her son enjoyed . . ."

"Very good Your Honour. How much did Giles and Jill suffer because of all the attention that you were giving to Tom might I ask Mrs Roberts?"

"Objection Your Honour . . ."

And I'd objected when Dr Heckman had asked that question, and insisted, 'I don't think they have suffered at all!' – 'Hmm, I wonder what your husband would have to say about that?' – 'He won't let me down!' – 'MRS ROBERTS IT'S YOUR CHILDREN I'M WORRIED ABOUT NOT YOUR

FEELINGS!' . . . but he won't let me down, he won't, he *couldn't!*

"Yes I was asked how much Giles and Jill suffered because of the time that I spent with Tom, and my husband was asked if my reply could be credited. But his reply, balanced as it was, was not credited by Dr Heckman who just continued his tirade . . ."

He's like a QC, I remember thinking that quite clearly, trying to trip me up on my own words. 'It can have a very deleterious effect on a child Mrs Roberts to feel he comes second in a parent's affections' – 'But I love them all equally!' – 'I *wonder!* You should enjoy Tom' – 'I never enjoyed a child more!' – 'THERE YOU ARE – YOU'VE JUST SAID THAT YOU LOVE THEM ALL EQUALLY!'

'Do you ever play with Tom? Do you ever tell him he's clever?' he goaded. But it was completely pointless even to attempt a reply, I don't think he paused for one anyway – just carried on ranting, 'Once, Mrs Roberts you told me that you spent all your time *working* with Tom – I've got it written down here in the notes. And I thought to myself when you said that, That is the most unfortunately child it has *ever* been my misfortune to meet.'

"Of course I should have said *playing* with Tom . . ."

* * *

And we played a little too, Dear Psychiatrist, with Dr Heckman, in a vain attempt to show ourselves unbeaten, resilient, in command of a sense of proportion, clear heads, humour (surely *musts* for parents of handicapped children) and perhaps naivety in our desperate attempt to set a lighter, more sane note so that we might achieve something in our time with this eminent psychiatrist who is *renowned for his work with children who have concentration and distraction problems.*

We had read a little of Dr Heckman's writings before we

went to see him. That is how we knew about his understanding of the term *hyperactivity*. It is also how we knew that he himself had devised a special term to describe the condition *over-protectiveness*. And the reason he'd done this, he explained, (strictly of course to fellow psychiatrists) was because parents were so good at reading notes upside down – the implication being that they then took exception to finding themselves so described. He'd written amusingly, and we'd been amused, so much so that in this vastly different arena we dared to ask (and I imagine we must have asked following on some apron-strings-pronouncement) 'Do you have a special word to describe parents such as ourselves?'

It seemed he swore at us in Greek[8] which wiped the smiles from our faces. And never again did I think of that article as amusing. For it suddenly seemed that if this judgement was being read upside down such a lot (a deduction clearly to be drawn from the text) then perhaps the judgement was being made rather too readily.

* * *

"Mrs Roberts, given that Dr Heckman might be expected – in the normal course of his work – to meet the full range of parents from the highly competent at one end to the totally inadequate at the other, his particular singling out of Tom (in respect of his parents) as *the most unfortunate child it had ever been his misfortune to meet* does make one want to ask . . ."

"Objection Your Honour . . ."

. . . No objection, no. But should we have shouted back? Might we not have achieved more if we had spoken our minds? At the risk of being labelled *difficult, pig-headed – don't touch this family*. (Plus the further concern that any behaviour perceived as difficult might rebound on Tom in some way.) Another fairly common condition requiring definition – *overcautiousness* perhaps? Characterized by swallowing insults, being flattened whilst trying and trying to find *what will help most – just carry on* . . .

"Oh yes, in the end my husband said, 'Surely you recognize that we have a child with many problems. Isn't it natural to want to help him? What would you do if, for instance, you had a child with only one leg?' 'Exactly,' said Dr Heckman, obviously delighted, 'I'd teach him to climb a mountain!' And that was particularly ironic because, you see, that's exactly what we thought we had been doing. Of course we didn't risk further acrimony by saying so, for I still had questions to put on behalf of Tom's teacher . . . but Dr Heckman wouldn't seem to answer, just looked pityingly as I struggled on, trying to convince him that there were *real* worries, that the teachers had *real* worries. 'And what can it do to a child,' I was finally driven to exclaim, 'always to be struggling yet still bottom? Might it not even be better to be top of an ESN?' Though of course I didn't really mean . . ."

"Mrs Roberts, could we please have the exchanges without editing?"

"Yes, 'Were you always top of the class Mrs Roberts?' Dr Heckman asked me. 'No, nearer the bottom!' I joked. 'And would you like to have been sent to an ESN school just because you were bottom of the class?' he threw back. And that was clearly so ridicul . . . sorry. I said, 'That's evading the question!'

"He leapt up at that, banging his fist on the table as he screamed, 'YOU COME HERE ASKING FOR HELP AND THEN REFUSE MY ADVICE! YOUR SON IS NORMAL MRS ROBERTS, NORMAL, NORMAL, NORMAL. THE ONLY THING WRONG WITH HIM IS HIS PARENTS!' He left then, slamming the door behind him."

* * *

Dear Psychiatrist,
That interview, along with the previous one that we had with Dr Heckman, was contracted in your report to 'Dr Heckman offered help and guidance'.

What *I* in fact received was three or four weeks of depression. I did of course bounce back. However, a vitriolic last word – precisely of the type we had been at such pains to avoid – was to remain in the notes to influence future thinking.

* * *

"So we might quite pertinently say, might we not Mrs Roberts, that Dr Hunt was extremely restrained in the one comment that he made in his Report to the Magistrates concerning . . ."

"Objection Your Honour! I really do protest most strongly at my Learned Friend's very evident suggestion that Mrs Roberts should be in some way indebted to Dr Hunt – the more so since his *restrained phrasing* is all part of that longer paragraph in which the intention is quite clearly to represent Mr and Mrs Roberts as parents who seek advice and then do not take it."

"Which I would estimate to be fairly accurate in this particular instance," said the judge, underlining some statement in his notes. "Did the recovery happen at seven as predicted?" he then asked.

"No, I'm afraid not. Tom certainly continued to do well – but not so well as to call it a recovery."

"In your opinion?"

"Yes."

"And how about other opinions?"

"Oh – well his welfare assistant, who had a lot to do with him, would have agreed with me, but the next doctor, our paediatrician's deputy in fact, whom we saw when Tom was seven years and one month, assessed his mental age to be about two and a half. She just wouldn't believe one single thing that I said about him. The Head Master, on the other hand, having completely dropped his line on a school for the educationally subnormal, continued to wonder about a school for the physically handicapped and called in the educational psychologist to advise. Mr Leroy, after testing Tom yet again, said to the Head Master,

'Though I have no wish to lumber you with children like Tom there is just no other place which could be doing more for him at the moment'. The school children – well mostly they enjoyed him as a great little character, but some thought him . . . different, I think that has to be said. And his teacher – well, as I have already indicated, she recognized Tom to have potential, but also many problems and she worried whether she had the necessary expertise to deal with them. So, by once again turning myself into an agitator, I managed to get the sessions for Tom with a Fairlands' remedial teacher that both Dr Heckman and Mr Strickland (the Fairlands' psychologist) had said he should have. She was a quite outstanding teacher, recognizing various problems which could, with guidance, be dealt with quite adequately in the classroom . . ."

"Excuse me Mrs Roberts, was this the remedial teaching that Dr Heckman was to have written to the Director of Education about?"

"No Your Honour, that was a separate recommendation. I think the reasoning was that the Fairlands' special teacher, having assessed Tom, would advise his class teacher *or* a remedial teacher, should one be supplied."

"Which of course she wasn't!" chipped in Mr Grey with a tired deliberation suggesting my tone unremittingly carping. And *his* tone was immediately picked up by Mr Shore, and rebuked. Leaving me to finish with Dr North, our paediatrician, who could have unqualified praise for his constant support (even though he didn't agree with Doman/Delacato either) and carefully considered – though not necessarily pleasing – opinions, for Tom's problems *were* too complex to be completely explained by Benign Cerebellar Dysphasia . . .

"He put Dr Heckman right on that?" queried Mr Grey.

"No, I'm fairly sure there was no correspondence between them. I think Dr North rather felt that they were duplicating each other's work. He suggested that we just continue to visit Dr Heckman."

"And not himself?"

"No."

"I see-e-e . . ."

"There really was no bad feeling – Dr North merely felt that Fairlands had the better facilities for Tom. He of course knew nothing about circumstances leading to our virtual excommunication from there."

So that now we would be under no one, unless I divulged the real situation and asked Dr North to keep us on, which was tempting. However, Tom, aged seven, was doing extremely well and should perhaps be seeing less of hospitals now.

* * *

Dear Psychiatrist,

Perhaps it would be both fair and appropriate to say here that one possible explanation as to the very varied assessments of Tom was a persistence of his own widely varying moods which could be noticed in looks, in behaviour and in performance levels. Thinking back I tend to remember the good days, even hours and minutes whilst a brief return to my diaries remind me of the difficult bits that came between. So, for instance, one night he might stammer over reading *if* and *but* and the next, select a book on Marco Polo and read it fairly fluently.

On some days he was completely switched off. On others he would bend his mind to weighty world problems following some news item that he had heard reported.

On some days he was loquacious and disarmingly polite and courteous as when he said to me, 'You must be so glad you married Dad, he's such an enjoyable man'. On other days he would be sullen and completely ignore people when they spoke to him.

Most of the time he was extremely disorganized, but just before his seventh birthday he told me who he would like to come to his party, what food and games he wanted then wrote the invitations and delivered them at school. (And when, on my birthday, he asked me if I would like him to make me a Penguin or a Koala cake, it was at least said with a confidence that promised a job done efficiently, on time and to the highest standards of a cordon bleu chef.)

On some days he would grasp the basics of being with a group of Giles' friends, showing fair dexterity in crossing ditches, scaling walls and talking rough. On others he would abandon the group and sit by himself in a dream, yet many of his comments indicated he was now longing for friendship.

His brother was his hero and led him with considerable patience into new hobbies and games. There was the inevitable cops and robbers stage then later he followed Giles into male chauvinism and became sadly intolerant of his sister's games which previously he had been happy to join (when the mood was right).

Occasionally a mood extended over a period of several days before it was replaced by its counterpart, at other times we might see several changes in one meal time. He might, for instance, start the meal lost in his own thoughts, then suddenly charge into the conversation which he would then totally dominate – until opting out again.

I found my mood exactly fitted his prevailing humour – though when his mood was low I almost certainly appeared otherwise in trying to initiate 'uplift'.

* * *

"Pray be upstanding . . ." for the judge. And the judge walks in with disquieting pomp – until I realize he can be made to look quite comfortable, like Father Christmas almost in his robes of red . . .

"We have in the witness box a mother who, I think we can at least say, has shown herself concerned for the boy whose upbringing is at the centre of this case.

"Now much of the earlier part of this hearing you will remember was taken up in trying to establish whether the young

Tom did, or did not, have certain problems that were likely to affect the way that he developed. And this was absolutely right because if he *did*, then a somewhat new complexion was going to be put upon what I would see to be the main message of The Heights Report (The Heights Report of course forming the chief substance of the Case for the Prosecution) and which I might summarize for you as follows: *that Mrs Roberts brought up her son in such a way as to adversely affect his development.*

"Hold that in mind while we go on to day two of the hearing by which stage it was quite apparent that the young Tom did have problems which were going to complicate the develop- mental process. It was also quite apparent that his mother had accepted the challenge that this brought, making considerable efforts to help Tom as she thought fitting. Was this fitting? The orthodox services by their carry-on-as-you-are – you're-doing- so-wells would seem to have thought so, at least at that stage. But was this necessarily the case? Remember Mrs Roberts seems not herself to have been totally persuaded, suggesting that *she* thought she might have done better. Could she have done better – given greater insight, understanding, things like that? From this distance of time probably impossible to tell. All that we can be sure about is that the orthodox services were without criticism – *until* she joined the Doman/Delacato whom she however found so helpful. So what perhaps we should ask now is *were* those techniques appropriate?

"Were those techniques appropriate? Given that we have now arrived at a stage where we have been told by a psychiatrist – and a very eminent psychiatrist – that Tom is normal, one very obvious interpretation is that the methods used by Mrs Roberts were absolutely appropriate. There are, however, various factors which would seem to spoil this view, the chief being that the parents themselves still feel there to be a problem, and to such a degree that the psychiatrist was actually provoked into emphasizing Tom's normality three times, and I quote, 'Your son is normal Mrs Roberts, normal, normal, normal!' That actually makes four which should make him very normal indeed. So is it just a difference of interpretation that we are looking at?

Clearly there was no coming together of opinion for the psychiatrist was finally driven to exclaim, 'The only thing wrong with Tom is his parents!'

"Now obviously in the light of the shortcomings that we are investigating this is a charge that we must examine very carefully indeed. So let us first be clear what it is that is wrong with the parents. In the psychiatrist's eyes, I think you will all agree, it is that they are looking at a completely normal child as one who had difficulties and clearly, if this was the case, then it was going to affect the way that he developed. So what is the truth? The Roberts might equally have argued that the psychiatrist insisted upon regarding as completely normal a child who *did* have many difficulties. Indeed, at the beginning of the consultation these difficulties were acknowledged, at least to the extent of Benign Cerebellar Dysphasia. He, the psychiatrist, did however go on to insist that Tom could expect to be free of the condition by the time he was seven – in one month's time. So, is it an act of faith he is demanding in declaring Tom normal one month ahead of time? Or are we to assume that the consultation took four weeks?

"Or might there yet be a third interpretation? Might it simply be that the psychiatrist is tending to overstate Tom's normality (or anticipating the recovery he expected in four weeks' time) in an attempt to persuade parents obdurately convinced of their son's difficulties to a more lenient view? Then of course there are the widely differing views of various other professionals which . . ." The judge's voice trailed off as he seemed to consider how best to deal with so many opinions . . . "which must be considered. Then again," he added, and frowning as he grappled with a further thought, "hasn't the debate rather moved on in the years since these consultations took place? Is it even permissible to use the word *normal* now – except in a wholly positive context? Who's normal anyway? Mr Grey?"

In steadily rising to his six foot height Mr Grey affirmed through every inch I AM. But it was Dr Heckman that he promoted – for his positive use of *normal.* (And also, his satisfied smile seemed to say, for his holding of manifold views useful to the prosecution.) His point made, he sat down.

Mr Shore rose, let his eye fall on his Learned Friend for a withering second, leant forward to add a word to his notes and then mentioned – now looking around the court – the paediatrician who had given Tom, at the age of seven years and one month, a mental age of two and a half. "Did you Mrs Roberts," he then added, "tell this doctor of Dr Heckman's views – expressed so forcefully just two months previously?"

"No – however, I did stress Tom's achievements. For instance, when she asked me what his language was like I explained that there were occasional confusions with tenses otherwise it was much like any other seven year old's, to which she asked me if he could put five words together yet."

"And that is what you'd expect a two and a half year old to do is it Mrs Roberts?"

"Yes, certainly a three year old. So, to *try* and impress her, I said he was reading quite well. She replied, 'Absolutely amazing isn't it! – Let's just see if he can recognize these pictures shall we?' And she handed him a thick cardboard book of farm animals, just one to each page and with words like quack, squeak and moo underneath. And that's a one year old's level – which of course didn't interest him at all. *And* she told me he couldn't possibly understand the way that I spoke to him!"

"I see, so that between one and the other . . . perhaps you were seeing too many specialists?"

"That's really what Dr North said, our usual paediatrician, and why – amongst other things – he suggested that we should stop our visits to himself."

"This was the paediatrician was it who considered Dr Heckman's diagnosis of Benign Cerebellar Dysphasia too simple?"

"Yes, that's right."

"But he also recommended that Dr Heckman take over the case?"

"Yes, though in fact we wouldn't be seeing him again either."

"So who are we left with – the educational psychologist, were you seeing him?"

"Occasionally, though of course we had been told to disregard everything that he said."

"But by a psychiatrist you are no longer seeing?"

"Yes, though he was still officially in charge of the case."

"Officially perhaps. However, if just one month after your last consultation he expected Tom to be completely recovered – was there any point?"

"Well he did indicate that good remedial teaching – which we expected him to organize – would be an essential part of that recovery."

"I see, but a recovery we can no longer expect to happen – at least in its entirety – in view of Dr North's later opinion?"

"Yes-s-s . . . I suppose that's correct."

"I see, so where does that leave us – the Head Master who now thinks Tom's problem to be physical?"

"Yes, but he did of course still think Tom to be a long way from . . . well *normal* I'm afraid was his word, and he was very anxious that I should understand this too."

"Presumably Dr Heckman's report to the school would correct this view?"

"No – no report ever went from Fairlands to the school."

"I see, quite fortuitous in one sense maybe in that the school would not have received the information that you were overprotective, wrong-headed and neurosis-inducing?"

"Yes certainly, but it would have been very useful if a report had been sent about Tom."

"Perhaps you yourself were able to convey Dr Heckman's opinion that Tom was completely . . . alright?"

"Well I did try to communicate various things which were explained to me by the Fairlands' special teacher, she . . ."

"One moment Mrs Roberts – I thought you said, or at least indicated, that Dr Heckman failed to fix this up?"

"Oh yes, but he had so insisted how beneficial such sessions would be that I managed to arrange for them myself."

"Ah yes, sorry to have interrupted, I think you were telling us how you conveyed this special teacher's findings to the school."

"Yes, she recognized Tom as a bright child with difficulties which could, nonetheless, be significantly reduced given the type of help that she demonstrated to me. However, though the Head Master was interested, he refused to accept as official a report coming through a third party."

"You being the third party?"

"Yes. He was very frustrated by the lack of *proper* information."

"I see, and continued to think of Tom as a long way from normal *mentally*?"

"At this stage yes, though it was the physical problem that he was concerned about in asking the educational psychologist's advice regarding the most appropriate school placement."

"The educational psychologist whose views we are disregarding?"

"Yes – but the Head Master had not been given that advice since no report ever went from Fairlands to the school."

"Oh yes – so we will stay with the educational psychologist. Don't I remember your saying that a decision regarding a school for the physically handicapped (which I imagine is what is being considered) was to have been made when Tom was eight or even nine?"

"Yes, that's correct."

"So are we to assume we have jumped a year, or even two?"

"No, I don't know why there was a change of mind, but Tom was just a little more than seven when he was tested again by the educational psychologist."

"I see, now what did he say to the Head Master? It was rather strange advice if I remember it correctly. I made a note of it somewhere . . . perhaps you could help me out?"

"'Though I have no wish to lumber you with children like Tom there is just no other place that could be doing more for him at the moment'."

"That's it! Very odd I thought. Did you overhear the remark?"

"No, the Head Master told me. He was so obviously delighted at the recommendation of his school that I don't think he was really thinking how it might appear to me. It's alright, I wasn't offended. He meant to reassure me that Tom was in the right place – and I took it in that spirit."

"I see, then we will! Which leads us to Tom's teacher who asked you to put certain questions to Dr Heckman, from which we might reasonably deduce that she was anxious to receive advice; advice which of course was not forthcoming from that particular quarter (at least not in a way that related to her questions), but which most certainly was from the special teacher, though only in the third-party form which she wasn't allowed to receive?"

"Yes, that is correct."

"Were requests ever made to Fairlands for information, either by the school or yourselves?"

"Yes, by ourselves many times. Similarly I had thought that his class teacher might be able to tell me things which could have been useful to the Fairlands' teacher. His class teacher, however, felt that she must get the Head Master's views on this. The Head Master said that he would not send a verbal report, though he would send a written one if officially requested. Unfortunately it never was."

"Did you request that it should be?"

"Yes, several times."

"Did the school themselves ever put in any type of request to Fairlands?"

"No, the Head Master always asked us to do that sort of thing."

"You didn't plead incompetence – being merely a third party?"

"No."

"So, to sum up, there was absolutely no communication between the school and Fairlands?"

"No – eventually the school doubted I was even taking Tom there, he had to miss afternoon school once a week you see, to attend the sessions with the special teacher."

"Thank you Your Honour, that is all my questions for now."

* * *

Dear Psychiatrist,

Tom continued in his own way, untroubled by what anyone, be they psychiatrist, teacher or contemporary was thinking. Perhaps it was this lack of awareness which found him out on the fringe, wanting companionship but not quite understanding the rules.

Though he was quite good at circumventing rules in his own interest; thus he could not get dressed in the morning as he was *invisible* and when threatened with the crocodile was *indestructible*. Exhortations and bribes proved ineffective so that I was finally reduced to more devious means. I accordingly gave notice of my intention to institute a system of penny fines for failure to dress himself within a given time. Tom got dressed immediately and later spent all his money at the sweet shop thus making it completely safe to be late getting up the next day.

And even had I docked next week's money he would not have suffered too badly, for he was adept at barter and at general dodges geared to ensuring he was in pocket; aged six he'd rubbed out the 1, 2 and 5 I'd chalked in the circles of a penny-rolling game and substituted 5, 10 and 50. He could even talk his sister into exchanging six one penny gobstoppers for his half-eaten liquorice chew, somehow persuading her that there was, 'One metre left'. And I could give many other examples of deals that went his way.

It was trading in more general talk that posed the problems. I peppered my talk with high-interest words to win his attention – usually to no avail, then, out of the blue, he would make some remark, joke or observation that just wouldn't have occurred to anyone else. On one such occasion he was laughing so much it was some time before he could convey to the rest of us the reason for his mirth; he had read the sign above a well-known shoe shop as *Free man! Hardy Willies*. The joke generally enjoyed and he switched off again. The Head Master said he was stubborn and wouldn't work to his ability. But I wondered about that *wouldn't*. Weren't there reasons that made that 'wouldn't' *couldn't*? Or *couldn't often*? 'Couldn't he sometimes sit with the other children?' – 'Definitely not, he wouldn't work!' – 'But wouldn't he be more inclined to work if he felt more like them?'

– 'No, it wouldn't work – having special children in ordinary schools only works if . . .' they behave exactly like ordinary children.

And now, to confuse the picture further, he developed a keen interest in a game that was in advance of most of those other children (so that he had to go to the top class every Friday afternoon to play it). A game requiring tactical abilities and total concentration – and he stuck at it for hours. I didn't teach him, to make some statement about his being too good for ESN school or something like that (because this was *before* that threat had been lifted). No, it just wouldn't have occurred to me to do so. His brother taught him and Tom learned all the basic moves in one night. His talk now contained quite technical reports, 'Giles moved diagonally and took my bishop but I set a trap and took his pawn' (he improved later on). The only sad thing was that his interest in flowers wilted as life became completely dominated by this CHESS.

* * *

"*Chess?*"
"Yes, chess."
"Tom played chess?"
"Yes – Tom."
"You really mean *chess?*"
"Yes – chess!"
"And this was aged . . ."
Speechlessness here overcame Mr Grey. The judge looked amazed. In fact he could hardly have looked more so if a king, queen followed by knights, bishops, castles and pawns had filed into the jury making two rows of . . . eight.

"Seven?" supplied the judge, continuing from where Mr Grey had left off.

"*Seven,*" said Mr Grey with an intonation suggesting that he had, in the meantime, seen a hole in the defence.

But it wasn't a hole. Just strategy. "No! It's got nothing at all to do with the *magic age of seven* because you see he was only six years, six months and two weeks when he first played."

"Six years, six months and two weeks – you say he played chess at *six years, six months and two weeks?"* Only Mr Grey spoke but it was evident that many might have echoed those words if not obliged to respectful silence. A respectful silence such as I had occasionally hoped to achieve in using the words (more usually when Tom was twelve, fourteen, fifteen) in attempting to quickly redress the perspectives of those who spoke to him in words of one syllable, spoke *of* him with serious understatement, wrote him off . . .

"Is it now received opinion that the young Tom *did* play chess?"

If Mr Shore had said, 'Is it now received opinion that . . . bishops can only think diagonally?' he could not have met more curious, sidelong glances, or a silence so total one might have heard . . . perhaps not a pin but maybe a chessman drop . . .

. . . and certainly a sheet of paper being drawn from a folder, which it quickly became clear was a vehicle by which a quite powerful move might be struck. It was, Mr Shore explained, a report written by a Miss Godden, psychiatric social worker, who had seen Tom at The Heights when he was fourteen years old. "And if it pleases Your Honour," he went on, "I would just like to read one section to the court now." And in anticipation of that pleasure he held the report up ready.

However, it did not please His Honour who ruled that happenings be taken in their correct time sequence. Mr Shore hesitated a moment, and then, with a look on his face as if his queen had been taken at the moment of checkmate, he put the report away and very reluctantly sat down.

With seven years to get through before that particular move could take place there was plenty of time for development and Mr Grey had *seized* the initiative with a will and with a hypothesis I must in some way dispute lest it lead now to overestimation of Tom's abilities.

And as so often in the past I longed for that diagnosis, that neat explanation which might have suggested some answers, insights, ways forward every time that I was asked to explain (and sometimes in the two minutes that were available) why it was he could do this and not that; see three moves ahead yet blank on the glaringly-obvious-right-under-nose; move straight or diagonally with appropriate and well-thought-out purpose, yet be quite unable to work out how to put on a pullover so that the V arrived at the front?

A *put-on* to amuse classmates maybe? He was quite a comic! One answer.

Perhaps.

And one overriding certainty . . .

"He really *did* play chess, not in a quiet contemplative way – for he never stopped talking (which had the distinct advantage of ruining his opponent's concentration). Even so he himself performed completely competently, keeping a hold on every piece and part of the game, and for how ever long that game took – perhaps an hour. However, in reality, little had changed, attention span still (or more usually) five seconds, which perhaps was the chief reason he so often couldn't get a hold on the quite ordinary things going on all around him, make predictions as to other people's actions; make friends that lasted more than five minutes. Then again, as he got older, different factors were to further complicate his development."

"Such factors as are precisely set out in The Heights Report, paragraph four, line four?" said Mr Grey, "And which are a clear development of one of Dr Heckman's chief findings!" he then added, in attempting to forestall the judge making any pronouncements about events being taken in their correct time sequence.

The judge, though not seeming disposed to be so easily satisfied, did pause to read the relevant section, saying odd words as he went. And everywhere people strained forward to catch, "Mrs Roberts . . . so overprotective Tom could not . . . as should . . ." He broke off to muse a while, his earlier caution replaced by a look suggesting that a way to a useful position had suddenly opened up. He looked down again to play this time with, "overprotective" and, "overprotective" and "overprotective as I see things". Take off glasses and clean, suggesting vision might have become somewhat blurred. Replace and peer again, "Yes it is all completely clear," he said, now confronting Mr Grey full-face, "it in fact states quite plainly that Tom couldn't develop as he should have done because Mrs Roberts was so overprotective that . . ." He stopped once more, perhaps seeing some obstacle to such seemingly simple suggestion . . . or perhaps he just wanted to make absolutely certain that he hadn't overlooked such an obstacle . . . before rushing on, uninhibitedly now, to read of an overprotectiveness so profound as to have checked development all across the board, particularly in the social field where, "Mrs Roberts' refusal to allow Tom to have friends, or to join clubs, has led to his solitary excursions to town and ultimately to the shoplifting of the chocolate Father Christmas which might be seen as a Cry for Help – and to my way of thinking," the judge raced straight on, "that means that if Mrs Roberts hadn't been so overprotective, well then Tom would have had friends, joined clubs, paid for chocolate Father Christmases and done everything else that is in the normal order of things! Do you have anything to say for yourself Mrs Roberts?"

"Well, I wasn't overprotective!"

"Oh – you are sure?"

"Yes Your Honour."

"Meaning you did allow Tom to have friends?"

"Yes Your Honour."

"At seven?"

"Yes, and all the way through to fourteen. The problem really was his own difficulties in making – and perhaps even more in keeping – friends."

"And that had nothing to do with your being so overprotective as to harm such attempts as he made?"

"No, Your Honour."

"However, that must be your own personal opinion!"

"Yes, though perhaps I might just mention that absolutely no one outside of the psychiatric departments ever used that term of me, furthermore – though it might be imprudent to say this – some people were fairly firmly of the opinion that I wasn't protective enough."

"I see-e-e . . . in what ways?"

"Well, in the area of friends for a start where I was criticized for allowing, even encouraging, Tom to be friendly with a boy (several boys over the years) who might have been a bad influence on him . . . and perhaps were, but good as well – especially when considering his desperate need of companionship!" Who was in a position to judge?

"And for a finish?" *the* judge prompted.

"Oh . . . well for a finish I suppose he'd never have taken the chocolate Father Christmas at the centre of this case if I'd really been overprotective – for I'd not have allowed such a vulnerable child to town by himself."

"So you're guilty anyway!" exclaimed the judge, "If not precisely as charged then certainly of a mismanagement that led to the same end result!" So saying he sat back squarely in his high leather-backed seat.

"But I wasn't *over*protective, and that was The Heights' main complaint".

"I see," said the judge, moving forward again more challengingly, "And you do realize do you Mrs Roberts, that in your assertion, you are not only contradicting The Heights – a serious enough thing in itself – you are also very much extending the case with all the extra burden on time and resources that imposes, because you see, if it could be quickly established that Tom's failure to develop quite as well as he might have done was simply owing to your being so overprotective as to not allow him to have friends, join clubs, things like that – well the case would be closed!" And as if to give encouragement to such a neat textbook conclusion he closed his file and put it to one side.

"I'm sorry Your Honour about the time and the costs (which I suppose might well be my own) but I simply cannot admit to this Heights' charge! Not only is it quite mistaken, I in fact spent so much time in exactly the opposite pursuit."

"In being underprotective?"

"Oh . . . well what I really meant was in encouraging him to join clubs, cultivate new interests, to make and – perhaps even more importantly – to keep such friendships as he started."

"So you failed!"

It wasn't a question, more a disappointed acknowledgement that there was no alternative but to continue from the seven year old stage, though he (the judge) had tried by every move, opening and strategy to engineer a more satisfactory outcome.

As I once had. 1) Make sure Giles has invitation elsewhere when Tom brings home friend, otherwise friend will go off with Giles. 2) Be discreetly on hand to remedy/prevent such Tom-preoccupations as might threaten games (i.e. his tendency to *fix* on some totally irrelevant and sterile detail, jeopardizing that which is relevant, productive and capable of mutual investigation) otherwise friend will persevere for a while and then go off by himself. 3) When friend goes off by himself attempt to re-launch Tom – or lay on refreshments and hope for a fresh start. 4) Check, double check and generally attempt to read four moves ahead to foresee possible pitfalls . . .

And Mr Grey was directed to continue with the questioning at this essentially productive time with developments on every front, mental, physical, emotional and social; for he *did* have one or two somewhat fragile friendships (even if he had to keep things going with gifts of his precious sweets) and he was also popular with teachers and classmates for being a character, having a certain comedian-ability which he quite shamelessly exploited . . . until he was eight years and two months when there was another type of development which I *must* outline, syllable by painfully stammered syllable.

"And you say it was the Head Master who got in touch with you concerning these worries?"

"Yes."

"Yet Tom had been suffering the same type of disturbances at home?"

"Yes-s-s . . ."

"You hadn't considered getting in touch with the school yourself about this?"

"No . . . I'm afraid not."

"And had anything happened at home to cause the disturbances?"

"No."

"So the trouble, we must presume, took place at school?"

"Yes – it was bullying in the school playground. Some of the children were driving Tom away from their games because he *trembled and looked funny.*"

"Mrs Roberts, excuse my interrupting, I don't remember your mentioning a tremor before!"

"No, it's odd, I never really noticed it until this point. It just affected his hands and was barely noticeable before the bullying started. I don't know what action the Head Master took once he realized what the trouble was, but it was certainly effective because there was no more trouble – at least for a year or so. The stammer stopped, his tremor calmed down and everything returned to normal."

"Oh good!" said the judge who then went on to propose closing the session at *this happy stopping place*, though he did allow Mr Shore one last point. "I would just like to add," Mr Shore added looking around, "that since it was the Head Master who got in touch with Mrs Roberts regarding Tom's troubles, rather than the other way round, Mrs Roberts can hardly be called *over*protective – can she?"

* * *

Dear Psychiatrist,

I'm not sure that the stammer ever got into the official notes, though I did make very particular reference to it when I gave the Case History to Miss Godden at The Heights for it seemed to me a clear example of the effect – motor through to emotional – that bullying and ridicule can have.

However, after the Head Master's intervention, things did progress happily for a time. And though Tom might have dropped such comic touches as putting on his pullover back-to-front, he did continue to treat the class to occasional impromptu humour. Even so, it does also have to be said that he was rather more sensitive to laughter from this point, and to situations that showed him up as different; the tremor – when it was commented upon, the table all to himself, the 'pay attentions' all to himself and the hundred and one situations that happened because he didn't – pay attention – all the time.

We could do nothing to stop the tremor, but we did try very hard to train him towards a constant listening state (with the object, ultimately, of cutting down the pay attentions) by making sure that conversations were of particular interest to him. Tom usually realized this halfway through, bursting in with a question which, for his deafness to the conversation thus far, was often comic, or irksome, or both. And yes we did laugh, and sometimes groan in the modified way aimed at alerting him to those situations where others might laugh, or groan, a great deal louder – if he didn't make listening a habit.

Which he couldn't do easily, so that he contrived other habits in attempting to get by in a world that seemed founded on talk, (and groans, and laughs). The question, for instance, which couldn't be answered unless you *had* been listening. Well you could just pretend that you hadn't heard the question and hope the questioner might move on; or, try repeating part of the question with a puzzled look, inviting further elucidation. If that didn't really help and an answer was now necessary, well – snatch at some response that had worked in the past; or make a guess from a key word in the question; or say you're not interested – they seemed to allow that.

And the talk might pass to something which you can join in, or follow at a distance, taking time out now and again to go up a sidetrack where you might miss the main view but get other quite novel angles – which you can expose, if you feel like it – or just listen in and try to make sense of what they were up to . . . before departing again . . .

So he might arrive at a particular stage a whole ten minutes after everyone else had left it, and before he'd had his say. Which he had anyway; new twists, odd reflections – conversation stoppers all . . . though it usually got going again. And he himself was adept at weaving the old topic into the new topic in a series of extraordinary connections.

So you found all this comical?

Oh no, the only laughs I heard were the ones I feared would happen if he didn't pay attention all the time.

* * *

"All rise . . ."

And hear how Tom rose to the juniors at eight (just one year late) as a completely ordinary member of class (which is to say that he did prove himself capable of working quietly alongside others, and without welfare assistant) and where he seemed so unspecial there was little to report – until the end of the school year when it was decided he had done so well that he should skip the next class to rejoin his age group in the Third Year Juniors where, aged nine and four months, he again saw an educational psychologist . . .

"If I might interrupt this flow for one moment Mrs Roberts," said Mr Grey dryly, "then I would just like to point out that this boy with – by your own definition – *so many problems*, has not only achieved junior status with all of the challenges that brings, but further has proceeded to pack two years of growing up into one to land in the Third Year Juniors and the first thing that is mentioned is an *educational psychologist* – is that normal?"

"Perhaps my Learned Friend should be apprized of the fact that an educational psychologist would almost certainly . . ."

. . . agree that progress was phenomenal – a view more or less in agreement with his class teacher's who recently had reported, 'Mental arithmetic and multiplication tables, one of three best children in the class – though at sixes and sevens in written maths. General knowledge good and always ready to get up and expand on ideas which are, however, far in advance of his ability to write them down'. He had though embarked on some lively stories of the once-upon-a-time-wicked-witch-casting-malevolent-spells variety, and which no doubt would have progressed through the thickening-plot-middle to the happily-ever-after conclusion if he hadn't written 'The End' mid-sentence and mid-spell (when, presumably, time ran out) so that . . .

" . . . we have been brought up short!"

"In front of a psychologist whose views we have been told to disregard!" put in Mr Grey.

"Oh no – Mr Leroy has gone! This was a Mrs Masters who was exceptionally good!"

"Good, bad or indifferent – essentially she's been brought in for problems real or perceived!"

But that wasn't right either, even the Head Master was quite without worries and at great pains to make this clear, "It was just felt that it would be a good idea to have a record of Tom's progress at this *particular point in time*".

However, though it was stated in The Heights Report that Mrs Masters had seen Tom at the ages of nine, eleven and fourteen, her findings were not mentioned, "The inference being," said the judge, "that the findings were not pertinent to the overall picture so that they should not delay us now!"

Further than perhaps to hear that her findings were probably of more significance than any other professional's, beginning with, "An IQ up fifteen points! In fact his verbal IQ was up 30 points, it being a 30% discrepancy in his visual IQ that dragged things down. But what had impressed Mrs Masters quite as much as the raised IQ was his determination to succeed, a deter-mination so enormous that a considerable degree of anxiety was added to those other factors that made it rather difficult for him to succeed, when in competition with other children that is".

"So why weren't Mrs Masters' findings included in The Heights Report?" said Mr Shore, "The profile of Tom being, at the very least, diminished by the omission, especially given that Mr Leroy's serious underestimation is the very first thing mentioned! Quite obviously," he continued, indignation clearly telling in his voice, "Mrs Masters' findings would have given valuable insight . . ."

As they had at the time, together with practical guidance on ways to meet his particular needs – in the newly discovered visual interpretation area, in the old attention span and hand manipulation areas. So, a writing fluency scheme, Mrs Masters having first established that this could be done without Tom feeling that he was being singled out for special attention, his sensitivity to such things being his, and his teacher's, biggest problem. 'Perhaps Giles could be encouraged to ask for help with his homework,' she suggested, 'to demonstrate to Tom that it's *not* a sign of failure to ask for help'. And I was invited to ask *her* for help, any time that I might have worries about Tom, 'He has done so well – and we do want to try and make sure that these gains continue!'

* * *

Dear Psychiatrist,
 I do realize that by the time we came to The Heights there wasn't a hint of the determination or of the imagination mentioned by Mrs Masters. I also realize that the official language of reporting would not allow *incredible progress* and *will to succeed* to be conveyed in anything like the pleased and animated way that it was to me. But surely the message was there, contained in such sentences as, 'Tom so wants to succeed that he refuses to ask for help, this being to indicate that he is having difficulties. Ways of coping with this were discussed with his mother and class teacher'. And when we came to The Heights we too talked about his one-time will to succeed, again not in an animated way, more wistfully, regarding things which by that time did seem incredible, even to us. For we too were affected by that expressionless face.

So that now, knowing how things came to be viewed, I am

tempted to overcompensate, to list the achievements of this fertile nine years' stage with determination and with imagination. However, that might just lead to a 30% overestimation, for his application was by no means constant. What would probably be more useful would be for me to give an extended view of Tom that takes in the many sides of his personality; a personality which, in the space of quite a short time, could have us exasperated, stretched, amused, taxed, wondering, challenged, beside-ourselves-with-laughter and always engaged.

Bill was going on an expedition to Zambia (Tom was eight at the time). One particular lunchtime we had talked about the animals he might see in the Luangwa Valley and also the protective injections he would need and Tom had seemed to sleep. The conversation moved to African illnesses I suppose because someone mentioned Bilharzia. At that word Tom sprang into focus with a question which, for his deafness so far, necessitated a résumé of much that had already been said, (this is when Giles and Jill switched off) the résumé itself being punctuated by many more questions. One of these questions was, 'If you went swimming in the River Luangwa would you get Bilharzia?' Bill started his answer, 'It's possible if . . .' or it might have been, 'It depends whether . . .' probably both in the course of the next few minutes for Tom liked definite *yes* or *no* answers and if he didn't get one just asked his question again, and again (now scaled down to, 'Yes but would you?'). Bill, on the other hand, felt that Tom should understand the necessarily variable factor of some answers and so, for a while, persisted with his *depends* and *it's impossible to be certains* until, thoroughly worn out, he said, 'Yes you most certainly would get Bilharzia if you swam in the River Luangwa between the hours of sunset and sunrise on a Saturday night'. Bill would have had no problem developing this theme, but that was not necessary because Tom had got his definite answer, its absurd nature possibly did not occur to him and certainly did not bother him. The conversation could now be resumed from the point where it had been interrupted some time earlier while Tom made what he would of his new information; a straight commitment to memory on this occasion – for three days later he repeated much of his learning to me including words like lethargic, parasitic (and Saturday night). He had also become in some way inspired (or infected) because, for a while, the subject became his chief interest; he poured over a parasite-book that we got from the library, asked countless questions and visited our neighbour to make an inspection of her drains and water butts.

This neighbour was enormously fond of Tom, as indeed were most adults who thoroughly enjoyed his unconventionality. Neither were they worried by his disinclination to sustain conversations beyond what was convenient to himself. (A disinclination which, on the other hand, was probably the chief factor behind his difficulties in sustaining friendships with children.)

We took Bill to Heathrow on the start of his journey to Africa. Unlike Giles and Jill, Tom seemed completely unaffected by his father's departure (though he was deeply engrossed in an ice cream) and I wondered if he had any concept of just what the departure signified. He put me right on the way back, 'Well Mum, if you die now we'll have to do all the cooking!'

A week later we received Bill's first communication, a minute log of the journey and of his first days in Lusaka where he described in colourful detail the people, the clothes, customs and the intricacies of the Zambian banking system. The children were all a bit fidgety before I had finished reading the six pages of close writing but Tom, in particular, heard me through with ill-concealed impatience before asking the question of overriding importance to him, 'Well Mum, what does he say about hookworm then?' I had to confess that hookworm had not got so much as a mention. Tom made no comment but sat straight down to a reply in which priorities were given due emphasis, 'Dear Dad. I hop that yow wont met a anicond or a sowlj panp' which rendered to standard English should read, 'I hope that you won't meet an anaconda or a soldier gang'. My only comment was to point out that he'd written the g's (of gang) the wrong way round. 'Oh that's alright Mum' he said, with the authority of one who has inside information, 'They all write left-handed in Africa'.

* * *

"The 30% discrepancy in the visual skills Mrs Roberts – what exactly did that mean?"

"Well, perhaps that he didn't quite see things as others saw them . . ." a phenomenon that the judge should, quite rightly, find interesting for what it might have to say about the discrepancies that can occur in witness accounts; the test being to arrange a series of pictures in their correct time sequence.

"So," said the judge thoughtfully, "The fire engine arrived before the fire had started, but he was ready with a good story!"

"Yes – and a story he couldn't be dissuaded from once he had decided upon it. It was hoped to tone down his imagination a bit so that he might come to see things as . . . most other people would."

"With nine-nine-nine consistency?" And *boring-ness* the judge's tone implied.

"Well it was in fact the imagination that went through a particularly fertile period for a friend he made around this time called Aran Allen, who had an even livelier turn of mind than himself!"

"He might actually have called the fire engine? Or started the fire?"

"Oh . . . they mainly went bird watching – and saw many rare and wonderful birds, most of them first sightings in this country."

"And was this encouraging the visual skills or adding to the 30% discrepancy?" put in Mr Grey dryly.

"Rather jolly whichever it was don't you think Mr Grey? Nightingales in December, cuckoos in January – Dear Sir, I heard a cuckoo on New Years Day. Is this a record?"

"With all due respect Your Honour, I think that might just require a 30% auditory discrepancy!"

The judge glowed as the perfect note was struck in a brief silly season where discretion flew and fancy held sway . . . while it could. "They must have had a wonderful time – a few threatened species as well! Mr Grey?"

Back to pigeons and crows. And the beginning of a long, hard wintry season.

Yet this had all started about seeing things the way that they were, so that I must try to explain how he came to see things around this time. Not things – Aran, through a 30% discrepancy – though that particular discrepancy was quite commonly held. "Aran was victimized – to do with his poor background I think. Tom, by his friendship, became victimized too. So he cut himself off. That didn't help so he joined those hurling abuse at Aran. That didn't help either but he still kept on . . . I'm afraid. But perhaps the most worrying thing was that he actually began to see Aran quite differently. And himself . . . which was, in effect, the way he was being seen by the other . . . *some* of the other children. The names had stuck you see."

"Oh dear," said the judge. And it seemed clear that his concern was in some small part owing to his earlier fun with cuckoos and threatened species. "Not everyone called him names – he was quite clear about that, (when he at last came to tell me). Some even wanted to be friends – but they were put off by the names, he was quite clear about that too." And fair, 'It would have made them unpopular you see Mum!'.

"It seems to me" said the judge, "That he was seeing things very clearly indeed!" And he put on his glasses, perhaps absent-mindedly, perhaps in some symbolic gesture, "Almost too clearly you might say". And he took off the glasses. I saw the irony . . .

And Jill's room, a mess of spoiled belongings and lipstick graffiti. I saw too the attempt to win friends by showing off . . . 'Don't you *see* Tom it doesn't work!' But it didn't work any other way either; everyone who came to the house came to see Giles. And he knew this, and told me then and there as we cleared up the mess – the hoped-for friends now gone. 'But at least Giles and his friends let you join in their games, if you want to.' And once a year he'd have friends of his own . . . 'Till the birthday party's over Mum; one boy who came was even a leader in turning everyone against me next day . . .'

"So what did you do?"

"We decided to go and see Mrs Masters."

"The educational psychologist!" said Mr Grey, managing to make the definition sound like a gross piece of name-calling.

"Yes – he really was *very* distressed!" And I stressed the 'very', I had to be more assertive now, that is why I was here. "And I couldn't go to his teacher, which might have been the more normal course, because it was the long summer holidays before I knew – he'd kept everything bottled up till there was this crisis and it all spilled out!"

* * *

Dear Psychiatrist,
You would have been surprised just how lucid Tom was once he did start to tell – all of those things that I'd realized for so long, but had thought he was unaware of. So why hadn't he told me before, as things happened? Well perhaps that would have been almost as bad as the real thing, a bit like announcing 'I'm a failure' (especially in divulging those names).

Much better to cope the best you can – that's what happens, yes, you somehow cope. Begin to think things couldn't be any different – that probably you are *odd, a failure* – even pretend you don't mind, and have this *sense* that life might be a whole lot worse if you do say something.

However, he'd told us now and obviously we wanted to change things. The trouble was he'd changed himself, in all sorts of ways that *he* thought would cut down the chances of failure, ridicule, rejection – but also perhaps of success.

* * *

"You surely didn't need a psychologist to tell you to do that?"
"No . . ." And neither had his very able teacher needed

alerting to the possibility of bullying when I saw her at the beginning of the next school term, "I'm just going through the points covered. Secondly, he needed to succeed at something".

"That shouldn't be difficult!"

"Sorry?"

"That shouldn't be difficult – if this psychologist's last assessment was correct! You seem to be trailing Mrs Roberts, let me remind you *enormous determination to succeed* – you were quoting . . ."

"Oh yes, he was translating letters into a code . . ."

'Do you know what a code is Tom?' – 'Yes I know morse and A is dot dash' – 'That's jolly clever! But in this code A is a square and B is a hook – look, there's the key and these boxes with letters on top need filling with the correct code-symbol, how many do you think you can do in one minute?' – 'The lot!' – 'No one's ever managed that before! Could you perhaps complete one row?' – 'Easy . . .'

"Are you communicating in code Mrs Roberts?"

"Oh, sorry – it was the whole way he'd set about the test that had demonstrated his enormous determination to succeed."

"And going on from there – *determination* to succeed, now he *needs* to succeed! Perhaps in some area more useful than a code?"

"But that was the problem, finding something he *could* succeed at."

"Presumably he could succeed at codes for a start!"

"Not really no, he knew he was being timed you see and raced through the test – but there were lots of mistakes."

"Some pursuit involving speed only?"

"No, his slight physical handicap put paid to that."

"How about chess?"

"No, it was so important for him to win that he'd given up things where it was possible to lose. If he was *obliged* to join a game he'd mess it up rather than risk losing. And that of course caused other problems which we also discussed with Mrs Masters. She said that it would be better to get him to work out why things had gone wrong rather than to tell him."

"Team sports – where there'd be less emphasis on the individual?" said Mr Grey, his own emphasis clearly managing to convey his dislike of the type of in-depth analysis just mentioned.

"Well he loved football but wouldn't play since some boys laughed at the way he kicked the ball."

"So he didn't play at all?"

"Yes – in the compulsory games."

Even Mr Grey fell silent here, while the Judge observed that the psychological test may well have demonstrated a strong determination to succeed, but that it rather looked as if that success would need to be in some field that was totally divorced from reality.

"Or competition! If we could have found something where competition didn't *have* to feature – Mrs Masters strongly recommended horse riding as a confidence-booster. However, when we mentioned it to Tom it seemed he wasn't interested."

"*Seemed* – he was talking in code too was he?" said Mr Grey having again found his voice.

Yes it had been a code of sorts, a code that had taken us around the sidetracks that border on dreams and nightmares, 'Tom would you like to have horse riding lessons?' – 'Actually Mum I'd like to drive a car!' – 'That's ridiculous Tom, you have to be seventeen to drive a car!' – 'Well that's a jolly silly rule!' – 'Of course it's not . . .' (get him to work out why) 'Responsible people have made that rule for very good reasons – can you think why?' – 'I don't know – the Porsche Carrera does 175 mph!' – 'That particular speed's against the law' – 'Well that's another jolly silly rule!' – 'Of course it's not . . .' (get him to work out why) 'Just suppose that a Porsche Carrera collided at 175 mph and . . .' – 'It wouldn't!' – 'It might! Look Tom, imagine this pencil here is you cycling down the path and just as you hurtle past the back door *here* Jill walks out. Now – will she be more hurt if you are travelling at 20 mph or 2 mph?' – 'I always know when I cycle past the back door that Jill won't walk out' – 'You can't possibly know that!' (Get him to work out why) 'I can because I'm ingenious!' . . . at dodging issues.

Until, at length, he lets drop why, 'I don't want to ride horses because girls do it and it's sissyish!' – 'But Tom several of Giles' friends go horse riding, you wouldn't call Jack, Harry and Warren sissyish would you?' – 'If Giles didn't like me for a day he'd spread it around school that I went riding and everyone would laugh' – 'I'm sure you're wrong Tom!' – 'No I'm not. Which do you think is best Mum, the Porsche Carrera, the Porsche Turbo or the Porsche Targa?' – 'The Porsche Turbo?' – 'Wrong Mum, the Porsche Carrera is faster and better in every way' – 'And what are the most important things in a car Tom? – 'Well I suppose safety and comfortability really'.

* * *

So, Dear Psychiatrist, perhaps there was some willingness to take on new and not immediately attractive (to a boy of ten) ideas, though we certainly didn't manage to sell the horse riding nor get him to see the illogicality of the reasons he stated against it.

'Stuck in a groove' was a term we often used to describe Tom's fixed notions with the 3+3=6 therefore 2+4 cannot also be 6 as one of its earliest manifestations. That he had moved on from there should perhaps have encouraged us as we determinedly attempted (6x6) to score the occasional plus.

* * *.

"Recovery would start with success!" Mr Grey put the solution in a sentence, "A success itself heavily dependant on the parents' ability . . ."

'Why won't you go to scouts Tom?' – 'It's too difficult' – 'But it's just one step on from cubs and you've done so well there!' – 'It's too difficult' – 'You can't know till you've tried!'

– 'I can, it's too difficult' – 'But . . .'

"He just *wouldn't* try anything we suggested! 'It's too difficult' became his standard reply and latest fixed notion – which of course was another way of saying 'I might fail'." And Mr Grey's look to the jury signalled 'the parents did'. "Oh, *the holiday just with Dad* – that was another of Mrs Masters' recommendations, and it was a great success. They climbed Snowdon."

"Ah, so he's climbed his mountain!" said Mr Grey in a clear reference to the Heckman taunt.

"Yes and by a quite difficult route too, which must have added considerably to the story when talking about it at school."

"Well certainly climbing a mountain would be counted an achievement in anyone's reckoning," said the judge.

Yes, an achievement in every sense, as were so many things he had done to this high – yet so soon to be eroded – point, and which must now be fully exposed, without pity. ". . . he was ridiculed you see, in a quite despicable way, by a teacher."

"For climbing a mountain?"

"No, perhaps it was more for some odd delight at seeing him crash head over heels to the bottom!"

And to laughter all the way.

But not now, for I had an audience who heard seriously how a teacher had walked into Tom's classroom one day and challenged, 'I'm brilliant at tables – ask me any you like and you won't catch me out!' And the children had responded enthusiastically to call, '9x9', '7x6', '11x12', '4x8' and the teacher was as good as his word. "Then Tom got up . . ."

"One moment Mrs Roberts, a trivial point perhaps but could you tell the court whether Tom *actually* got up on his feet or whether it is merely a figure of speech that you use?"

"Oh, I think he did – yes I'm sure because . . ."

"It was a school where the old values of knowing tables backwards and respect for elders was inculcated?"

"Yes, certainly."

"Please continue."

"Yes, well Tom got up and asked '6x8' – and of course he

was good at tables, mental arithmetic in general really, which makes the mockery that followed even worse for being so . . . unjustified."

"Mrs Roberts I hardly think that the present company require lessons in passing judgement!"

"Sorry no, but what I must say is that the teacher didn't answer Tom in the way that he had all the others, he simply said, 'Bet you don't know the answer to that Roberts, 48 – sit down!' And I might add that not only *did* Tom know the answer, he also knew something about the cheap joke since he said to me, 'He only did it to make the children laugh Mum because he said 48 very quickly before I had time to show that I knew'."

"Mrs Roberts, is it possible he might have . . . imagined this gibe?"

"Oh no, his indignation, the words he used were all too real! And there were two other *incidents* he told me about that were just as bad – on the third occasion he was ridiculed in front of the whole school."

"But Mrs Roberts how could it possibly get to a *third occasion*? Surely you would make your views known to the teacher in question immediately after the first!"

"No, Tom told me about all three incidents together, and by that time the teacher (who fortunately wasn't the class teacher that Tom had most of the time) had left the school."

"And prior to being told you hadn't noticed anything amiss, stammering, something like that?"

"No stammering no, and no worsening of the tremor that I was aware of. A worsening of his behaviour *perhaps* which could well have heaped further problems upon himself – and from the very same teacher."

"So what did you do – when you did hear?"

"I think I felt sick."

But the gut reply was no testimony to good parenting. "Surely this was the time, of all times, to find that something that he could be good at!" pressed Mr Grey. "Perhaps," responded Mr Shore, "he could have been led up another mountain ready to be knocked down again". And he was put down by the judge for a bad-sounding jest. "Surely there was something that he could be good at?"

Well he *was* good at tables, one of the best in the class, and at mental arithmetic, and at general knowledge and know-how where he was always ready to get up with answers, ideas or whatever . . . .

Until this teacher walked into the classroom one day who was brilliant at spelling.

'Bet you don't know how to spell that Roberts, C-H-E-M-I-S-T-R-Y.'

Sit down.

Stay down.

Say nothing.

"Have you nothing to say Mrs Roberts?"

"We didn't find anything he could be good at, no. But we did encourage the friendship which started up again around this time, with Aran."

* * *

But he was brave. Certainly he was good at being brave – I can see that now Dear Psychiatrist. For just going to school each day without fuss or complaint, without ever holding back, *must* have taken some courage. Only once did he try to malinger, 'I've got a headache, earache, foot ache and soon I'm going to have a toothache so I can't go to school!'

His friend Aran had rather more guile in dodging threats, or mouth and brawn in meeting them full on. He also had a father who would occasionally weigh in on his behalf. It was Tom's fervent wish that we too would forcefully take on the parents of particular troublemakers and our preference for talking-it-though diplomacy was a sad disappointment to him. It was possibly also another reason why we heard so few of his worries. He'd cope on his own. Just carry on.

Which he did very satisfactorily, getting quite good reports from his class teacher throughout his last year at primary school. Though it does also have to be said that in common with every other teacher he'd thus far had, she found it very difficult to assess his ability, never knowing whether she was pushing him too hard or not stretching him enough. A little mild cajoling was useful and a threat to give him an easier exercise if he didn't *get on* was sufficient to trigger a burst of activity and finished work.

Except on one occasion which very much worried this teacher. She had announced at the beginning of the school day that each pupil could do *some exciting experiments with balloons* once a certain amount of set work had been done. Anticipation of such congenial occupation was sufficient to completely destroy Tom's already fragile concentration and he was quite unable to give his mind to the set work. She, while appreciating the problem, felt that she must stick to her original directive. The result was that Tom went home at the end of the school day not having touched the balloons (though he mentioned nothing of this to me) and the teacher went home feeling wretched – and very much in need of specialist advice on managing this type of circumstance.

The Head Master, viewing Tom from the perspective of one who had seen him through six years of primary school, could talk about enormous advances all across the board. 'When he first arrived he stuck out like a sore thumb. Now, if a visitor were to walk into his classroom, they wouldn't know anything was amiss.'

Unless they happened to follow, unseen, to the playground where different rules allowed that differences would remain.

To diminish again back under the eagle eye of his teacher. She told me there had been a cruel lot of boys in the class – and there had been *incidents* when her back was turned. Mindful that this sort of pattern was likely to continue, she strongly recommended that he go to a secondary school where there would be a softening female presence.

Though of course it was to be an accepted member of the male group that he craved, and from which he sadly stuck out like a sore thumb – however inconspicuous he tried to be. For it was from this point that he quite definitely adopted a policy of keeping quiet in the presence of other children (I was given strict instructions never to address him in these circumstances). It was a strategy that brought no more success than the flinging-mud-at-Aran had done – in an attempt be be in the gang. But he did, for a while, have a few more comradely escapades *with* Aran.

* * *

"The boy who collected so much abuse!" said Mr Grey, taking shocked tactics from his repertoire.

Tom's choice had been between being bullied with a friend and being bullied without a friend.

This time he'd stuck by Aran with staunch loyalty.

"You encouraged this?"

"Yes."

"So please let it not be said," put in Mr Shore, "that Mrs Roberts did not allow Tom to have friends!"

"Perhaps we should just hear what guided Mrs Roberts in her thinking," said the judge, his brow a maze of questioning furrows.

"Oh . . . mainly that Tom was so desperate for friendship and this one was, in many ways, a resourceful one." Judge frowns as if football had just come through his front window and waits, pen in hand, to mark down my words. "Together they collected all manner of things, stamps, conkers, sweets – from several kindly disposed people," (not to mention black looks from others, tickings off, left over beer after village hall parties), "frogspawn, marbles, 007-type adventures," ('Listen Dad this really is true, we were in this wood and a man pointed his glove at us and a spark came out') "football cards, football jokes, football dreams," ('Hey Mum, Aran's got this aunt in Argentina and if you can pay for us to go we can watch the world football . . .') "to ridicule and blame, some of it deserved, some of it not. We eventually felt obliged to confine them to barracks and tried very hard to initiate activities that would interest them within our house and garden. But that was altogether too limiting for an independent spirit like Aran so that he stopped coming."

Judge looks very relieved and adds a line to his notes with firm crossings of T's and dottings of I's as if to make abundantly clear his liking for order over threatening chaos.

But Tom was again at a loose end, and unwilling to do anything more challenging than to bounce a football, then catch it, time after time, after time.

Once upon a time, when he was eight, he suddenly reversed a game of chess that we were playing by six moves in order to demonstrate to me what a stupid move I'd made at that point. Disoriented and convinced the game was now wrecked, I didn't benefit from the instruction (though I do remember being told that I was very fortunate to have someone of his standard to play with). The instruction over and he returned the pieces to the positions that they had occupied before he had interrupted the game. He could now win and I could marvel at this previously unrecognized skill.

'Chess Tom?' – 'I'm not interested in that sort of thing any more'.

* * *

Dear Psychiatrist,
I should perhaps give an example of Tom's writing in my Case History. It is some work that he did at home late one night, remembering only at the eleventh hour that he had to write a poem to hand in the next day. Having remembered he sat straight down and poured it out. He forgot to hand it in which is why I still have it.

The One Eyed Boggler is cunning and brave
When he has seen someone he'd make them his slave.
He is never a coward, and always high powered
When I see him he chases me and I run to my house,
He tries to blow my house down puffing and panting does he.

Beware my son! He's as hungry as wolves,
He's cleverer than five hundred packs of fools.
His eye is as big as a saucer and he's got
Ten lasers fifty times more powerful than razors.
And as fat as a windmill is he.

He was eleven when he wrote it, and longing to be invincible.

* * *

"Be upstanding . . ."
Obediently I rise, whilst in every other way sinking. The halfway stage, primary to secondary; eleven plus. Mr Grey bows peremptorily, impossible to imagine deference or a wig skew-whiff. But the judge, still in reassuring red, talks expansively about important landmarks, widening horizons, opening doors . . .
And he had to go through one of them, come what . . .
". . . may be appropriate to remind ourselves what a test this will be for *any* child . . ."
Mrs Masters had said that as we'd met with the Head Master to discuss the move, meaning to reassure me that *initially* every child would be tested – that is to say those who would quickly *connect*, to stride effortlessly ahead again, and those who would have an enormous struggle just to stay . . .
". . . put another way we must surely concede that his achievements to this point have been quite remarkable, especially when bearing in mind the extreme pessimism which attended his starting school. Yes, I think that we can all say, and with

good reason, that Tom has achieved Eleven Plus with flying colours – Mr Grey?"

"Thank you Your Honour, and might I first add my applause Mrs Roberts for this undisputed success!" So saying Mr Grey bowed – then continued, "The onus on you to find just the right secondary school must have been very heavy indeed!"

"Certainly."

"What were the precepts that guided you?"

"Oh . . . well of course we wanted very much for him to be happy, to achieve his potential, that sort of thing. But really . . . I just have to say that we hoped he'd be able to cope and not be bullied too much."

"You just hoped he'd be able to cope!" Mr Grey's stressing of the clipped-off sentence as he studied me through narrowed eyes seemed to suggest the meanness of my vision; but I saw all those doors and heeded many and well-informed views. 'Demands on *any* child his first term are quite enormous, and Tom has done so well – it could all be lost if . . .' , '. . . staff/pupil ratio so drastically cut – any little problem might go quite undetected if . . .', '. . . must also bear in mind that his distractibility problems will be much harder to accommodate, *here* his one class teacher can often adjust to his needs, at secondary school . . .'

"Never mind!" Mr Grey tired of waiting for an answer, "Your second precept, *you hoped that he wouldn't be bullied too much,* you thought, did you, Mrs Roberts that just a little bullying would be character-building?"

"Objection Your Honour! Does my Learned Friend mean to build Mrs Roberts' character by such bullying tactics?"

Or to render demoralized, ineffective, an easy target. "I'm sorry, what I *should* have said was that we didn't want him to be bullied at all. However, realistically, the chances were very high that he would be,[9] and this was the view too of his primary school teacher and Head Master, also of Mrs Masters – all of whom we went to for advice on the secondary school situation."

"So what did they advise?"

"They didn't actually recommend a particular school, but

went through the various options that were open to us."

"Which were?"

"The local comprehensive first I think. But Mrs Masters warned that could be dangerous, the large classes militating against the child who might be struggling, and the sheer size of the school making it easier for bullying to go on quite undetected."

"So you were looking for a small school, with small classes and a high teacher/pupil ratio?"

"Yes, and where there would be sympathy, in the very widest sense, for a child who might have problems."

"So?"

"There was a prep school which perhaps fitted these conditions. But of course, being a prep school, it would only have been a possibility for two years, which we felt might well be two years amongst boys cramming for public school entrance at thirteen. And that suggested the sort of competitive atmosphere that we most wished to avoid (and in the all-male environment that we had been told would be bad). Then again we didn't really want Tom to have to face another move at thirteen because of the enormous stresses . . ."

"That moves involve, yes, yes Mrs Roberts, I think we all understand," said Mr Grey who nonetheless then proceeded to question everything that I'd said and in such a way as to clearly declare, *overcautious, fixed attitudes and by this you were very much limiting your options.*

"I think what Mr Grey is saying Mrs Roberts," interposed the judge, "is that for you, and of course Mr Roberts to have held so many strong views and reservations might eventually have resulted in there being nowhere for Tom to go at all. However, presumably he did go somewhere," he continued, looking upwards as if chasing some new thought, "and exactly where we shall no doubt in due course hear. So, is it actually necessary to . . . no!" he said decisively and now looking straight at Mr Grey, "No, I suggest that we let Mrs Roberts set out the options quite unchallenged then, once the choice that was finally made is announced – that will be the time for you to come in with your objections, if you have any!"

And there was considerable amusement that it had even been suggested he might not. However, for the moment, I gave the options unchallenged and more or less as they were discussed that afternoon, the qualifications and reservations not merely my own, nor the recommendations unanimously agreed, (though there could be said to have been agreement on those options which would, in all probability, be very unwise). For Mrs Masters' clear favourite was thought *the worst place possible* by his class teacher and his class teacher's recommendation was thought *a potentially dangerous place* by Mrs Masters – also by the Head Master who did not, however, state a preference. But the class teacher backed my (our) choice, if with enormous reservations (which we shared too) though probably prudent not to divulge all that now . . .

"So we might be said to have everything from purpose-built at the one end to high-risk at the other" said the judge when I had finished, studying his own sketch of the possibilities, which he then went through again, carefully setting out the advantages and the disadvantages of each move. "Quaker, independent, (though authority will assist) strong on pastoral care and very sympathetic to special needs – though not a possibility until thirteen. Boarding too, perhaps not quite the threat Mrs Roberts feared, things would have changed since her day! Physically handicapped, again excellent care and facilities, high staff/pupil ratio – though clearly inappropriate, considering how relatively minor the disability. Then of course there was the local comprehensive where problems attendant upon large numbers and high pupil/teacher ratio have been fully outlined, presumably the same at other comprehensives. Which just leaves what would almost certainly have been the most unattractive option of all as far as Tom himself was concerned – that he should stay put in his primary school for a year. So where did you send him Mrs Roberts?"

"Oh, after much thought and a visit to the school to explain about Tom's particular difficulties, and to satisfy ourselves on one or two points, we chose the local comprehensive."

"The one described as potentially dangerous!" said Mr Grey

with such an appalled disgust as must have persuaded everyone that we had made both an irresponsible and an ill-judged move.

"Might I with your permission Your Honour," said Mr Shore with a little bow, "point out to my Learned Friend that Mrs Roberts did say the local comprehensive and not the lions' den. It furthermore seems probable that any choice that was announced would have drawn the same vehement response."

"That may well be," said the judge, "however it is significant, is it not, that Mr and Mrs Roberts chose the one option that actually had the label *dangerous* attached and, as far as I can remember, nothing to recommend it at all."

"Oh but there were things, I'm sorry I forgot to mention them before. The Head Master had impressed us a lot – though perhaps I should say that he was concerned about taking a child whose difficulties might be greater than his school would feel happy to cope with. But you see such concerns would probably have worried any school that we approached, and this one did have some advantages that the others couldn't have.

"Such as?" said Mr Grey, looking very doubtful.

"Mainly through its links with the primary school that Tom had been to, perhaps the greatest of which was that he would be moving with children he knew."

"And with children who had been bullying him!"

"No, as luck would have it, the chief culprits were going to other schools."

"Good! So we have luck on our side. Now tell me Mrs Roberts – did this move work?"

"Well . . . he wasn't bullied as far as I know. But no, I'm afraid not."

* * *

Dear Psychiatrist,
The actual change from primary to secondary went very well, Tom managing to find his way around the school to arrive at the

right place, at the right time, at every change of class. 'It was,' he told me his first day home, 'a lot better and a lot easier than primary school'. But so far they had done little more than receive new exercise books.

I confess to feeling considerable anxiety myself, this having a lot to do with the passing from the friendly familiarity of the primary school with its happy pictures and once-upon-a-time stories to the vast unknown of the secondary set-up; fairly well represented by those pristine exercise books, just bearing subject-title and teacher-name and towards all of which I seemed only able to extend a fingers-crossed sort of hope.

Except where homework was concerned. Now every evening was spent in organizing and helping Tom to do it. Sometimes a certain amount of research was necessary in order to decipher the instructions in his homework book. One night, for instance, he had written down for geography, 'Describe how insatable and can be reclaimed for farming'. That should of course have read, 'Describe how unsuitable land . . .' and considerable time was spent in working that out and then in trying to establish what they had talked about in class – or giving the type of instruction that might dislodge some half-caught seed: 'Oh that's it Mum! Poor land in Africa, hard land in Japan, ice on the mountains'. And there we met more stony ground, which *might* with careful tending reap . . . 'Hurry up Mum – I want to listen to the charts!' Rockier still. But he did have a point – half an hour had gone by and he hadn't written one word of what was supposed to be a twenty minute exercise. (Another serious disadvantage was his lack of any friend whom he might call on for clarification of these homework conundrums.)

* * *

The judge, having established that Tom *managed* for just one year at his first secondary school, remarked that questions centring on various aspects of unsuitability would no doubt have to be asked. He then looked in his notes before adding, "However, I think that we should allow that the parents' choice of school was probably made in good faith, in that Tom's success at the local primary no doubt led to their making the assumption that success could be expected at the local secondary too. Mr Grey do you have any questions?"

"Yes," said Mr Grey smartly, "presumably Mrs Roberts *good faith* was not going to be sufficient for your second secondary choice?"

"Objection Your Honour. Given the choice that Mrs Roberts has already outlined I would think that good faith might be required in very large measure."

Mr Shore allowed himself a quiet smile amidst much more wholehearted amusement. But the judge didn't laugh, possibly because he felt that his own words had been trivialized, or maybe because he suddenly saw the need to inquire into just why the good faith had been so ill-founded. For he called for order and then asked why it was that Tom had failed at secondary school when he had apparently succeeded at the primary level.

"Oh several reasons. But mainly I think because of the number of subjects that suddenly had to be taken and each one taught by a different teacher who cannot possibly get to know him in that special way which makes such a difference, and as his one primary school teacher most certainly always did."

"I see-e-e . . . Nonetheless one might expect many others to bow under this same pressure!"

"Yes, but more normally they will be the ones who have problems with reading, writing and arithmetic – then they can be put in the remedial class."

"Oh I see! And Tom can read, write and calculate quite well so will not fit this more normal grouping?"

"Yes, that is right."

"Other types of difficulty didn't qualify for special help?"

"Yes, in theory. In practice budgets and cut-backs meant little could be done."

"Unless I suppose the difficulties happened to over-lap . . . didn't you once spend considerable time yourself helping him with – shall we call them the *three R subjects*?"

"Yes-s-s . . . but because I thought it would help him to cope."

"Whereas you've put him in a position where he's *got* to cope!"

"Yes. Furthermore, because he could read and calculate quite well, the deduction was *occasionally* made – following on some sub-standard piece of work – that he couldn't be applying himself properly. Which had the effect of making me feel I had actually done a *dis*service to Tom, and also to his teachers, in creating such a seeming dilemma. I felt wretched about it all."

"Oh I don't think that's quite right! In fact Mrs Roberts I think I would go as far as to say that in order for this case to work you must be totally biased. In other words you must argue with conviction that any failings were entirely the school's fault."

"But I really *couldn't* do that! You see many of the teachers were enormously concerned and put in a lot of time and effort trying to help."

"And he *still* had difficulties?"

"Yes-s-s . . . well it wasn't quite straightforward; you see in a large class there wasn't much that could be done in a lesson. However, some teachers, recognizing a child with difficulties but also with ability, gave up their break-time in order to give him the individual help he so obviously needed. This of course meant Tom giving up his break-time too, which didn't particularly please him, especially as other teachers, not under-standing him at all, were keeping him in to re-do what they considered to be poor work. And the poor work, I think it's fair to say, was sometimes a case of his handwriting completely disintegrating under the sheer pressure of it all. In the end I think he just gave up."

"Presumably you were able to explain all this – once you had worked out just what was going wrong?"

"Unfortunately Mr Hunnisett, head of junior school, to whom we had to do the explaining, was one of those who felt the problem to lay entirely with Tom."

"Oh dear. Do you have any questions Mr Grey?"

"Yes Your Honour," said Mr Grey springing up with the speed

of one who has felt restrained too long. Or perhaps of one who felt the judge to be showing sympathy too easily for the various explanations that I had thus far given, prompting him to take an opposing and much tougher line, and one that seemed uniform with (or at least in sympathy with) the head of junior school (whose interest was to pull into line a pupil who was not meeting the educational standard expected of him; not even in a school sympathetic to, and well-briefed in, his difficulties and whose very purpose was the comprehensive education of *all* levels of ability – assuming, of course, a certain minimum standard). "So why was it," Mr Grey eventually asked, "that Tom *was* having such difficulties – given that his IQ put him well above the lower level of ability?"

"Largely because of his problems with concentration . . ."

"But Mrs Roberts," said Mr Grey with a look of *you really must do better next time*, "the school must have been very used to butterfly minds!"

"But it wasn't a butterfly . . . sorry, but to me that's something quite different, there were neurological reasons why . . ."

"Or could it simply be a case of him not applying his mind?"

"Objection Your Honour! Has my Learned Friend perhaps lost the ability to attend for more than ten seconds to the facts? Other than that the reasons behind this particular attack must remain completely *incomprehensible!"*

'Certainly he's capable when he tries, here's a good piece of work and a bad piece of work,' said Mr Hunnisett holding up two pieces of writing that should underline his lesson. But the first was obviously straight copying from the blackboard, he'd even written *leave 8mms for the margin* and I couldn't point that out without seeming to insult Mr Hunnisett and making Tom appear even more at sea. 'I think the *bad* piece is partly pressure of time, his handwriting . . .' – 'But Mrs Roberts, in a mixed ability class he is being compared, at the bottom range, with children on the ESN border – and he's not doing as well as that!' Clearly coordination/concentration problems counted for little so perhaps I should pursue the social line, 'Does he have friends?' – 'I'm afraid only those who see in Tom someone they can push into trouble and then run away when he gets caught. There is no one who will stand by him. So what are we going to do?' – 'Is there no way he can drop one or two subjects and spend more time on the really important ones?' – 'Mr Roberts – in a school of eight hundred and fifty we really can't start writing individual programmes, unless we're allocated more staff. No, we've done all that we can, I would suggest that you . . .'

"A *pep* talk! Does my Learned Friend really feel that for Mr and Mrs Roberts to have given Tom a pep talk would have . . ." And there Mr Shore's words fell away, as if at his utter incredulity that such an idea could even enter the thinking.

Tom had found it hard too, even distressing. He *was* working the best he could, had dozens of friends. Most of all he didn't want to move school.

But he had to. Mr Shore said that the onus on us to find just the right school must have been even heavier than the year previously and ran through the available choices, the prep school – but only now for a year, the quaker school – but not *for* a year, the school for physically handicapped – but . . .

* * *

The trouble was, Dear Psychiatrist, that Tom insisted he liked it where he was and became very distressed whenever a new school was mentioned. He'd do well in the exams – that would show them! 'Help me revise Mum!' So a week's crash course in everything from geography to french and which reverberated through strained relationships, shattered panes and poor results. 'I'll do better, please don't move me!' – 'But Tom, surely you can't be happy when it's all such a struggle?' – 'Yes I am and it's not a struggle!' – 'But the teachers say . . .' No, I can't possibly say that.

But he saw it all – to even further distress – when he opened his report on the way home from school.

'Must concentrate harder.'

'Appears to have more ability that he is prepared to use.'
'Little understanding of space or shape.'
'Quite honestly I don't know what to say!'
'Class work untidy and careless.'
'Impermeable to reason and persuasion.'
'Always gives of his best in a subject where he has very little ability.'
'I'll do better Mum, *please* don't move me!' and please don't move us in our essential search to find somewhere that is willing to take a boy who has failed academically, who is distressed and showing signs of emotional disturbance (so how can we even ask anywhere) and who is likely to be further distressed and disturbed by that move (so how can we ask it of him). But – he cannot stay where he is.

* * *

"Mrs Roberts, before Mr Grey continues, could you just tell me, did Tom have free school dinners?"

"No Your Honour, I think he took sandwiches."

"*Sandwiches!* Then that might explain it – according to a radio programme on matters educational that I heard last night, a child has to have free school dinners in order to qualify for special teaching help."

"Oh no Your Honour, I think that's how special teachers are allocated, so many children on free school dinners will earn one. But it's not necessarily the children on the free meals who get the teaching."

"You mean a child on sandwiches who happens to need teaching help might get that help so long as there are enough children on free school meals to achieve a special teacher?"

"Yes Your Honour, at least I think that's how some authorities calculate need nowadays. It was different when Tom was at school."

"Oh of course, you had to be below standard at reading and writing then."

"At his first school. At the second school that Mrs Masters found for us the child could get just such help as was necessary in a Resources Unit. The rest of the time he, or she, was in the main part of the school which was a normal comprehensive."

"And all this irrespective of reading ability, sandwiches, things like that?" said the judge, waiting pen in hand for my answer while a juryman looked very pointedly at his watch as if he would have settled for the sandwiches (or at least something more substantial than the make-believe so far served) just so-long as some progress might be made. Which it certainly was for I explained that a child with a reading difficulty might well go to the unit for help, as might a child with a heart condition, but in that case only perhaps for alternative occupation during games periods. "It was absolutely according to need," I finished, with then an afterthought mention of the Warnock Report's[10] recommendations for children with special needs-teaching. "It was the sort of unit that they suggested should be set up quite generally in comprehensives."

From fairly general blank looks it appeared that most had not heard of Warnock (nor of units being set up quite generally). However, proceedings were not held up over that, for Tom was in the right place, the only disadvantage being that place's far distance – so, long journeys and no out of school activities. "It does just occur to me," said the judge, "that ideal though all of this sounds, it was going to involve Tom in the type of special help he so much resented!"

"Yes, that is right, and it was a problem. However, there was a quite amazing person in charge of this unit – a Mrs Johnson – and Tom took to her immediately."

"I see. Such a person as might have been recommended by Warnock," said the judge, beaming his satisfaction around the court. "Do you have any questions Mr Grey?"

"Thank you Your Honour. So Mrs Roberts," said Mr Grey, rushing on all in the same breath, "Tom regained his confidence, picked up lost ground and worked more and more in the mainstream?"

"I object Your Honour," said Mr Shore, quickly reading my

own loss for words, "my Learned Friend would make it all as easy as the receiving of free school meals."

"I would have to argue with you there," checked the judge, "apparently it's enormously difficult . . ."

'I'm rubbish at everything!' – 'Not at doing yourself down you're not!' – 'Have you seen my report from the other school?' – 'Yes, I just loved your music teacher's comment!' – 'Some people are brilliant at everything. I'm rubbish!' – 'So you've insisted before, quite incorrectly – that piece of work's good for a start!' – 'Do you mean it's good, good average or just good for me?' – 'Have you been reading the psychology books?'

"The trouble was his low confidence," I said, in being eventually required to explain why recovery wasn't as simple as the receiving of free school meals (if indeed that was simple). And to give some idea just how low Tom's confidence was, I explained how he had answered when Mrs Johnson had praised some work as *good*. "And if in reply to that Mrs Johnson had said *good* or *good average* he just wouldn't have believed her."

Which left *just good for me* as everyone worked out altogether and wondered – with the judge – how things had progressed from there, and laughed – as had Tom – at the psychology book retort.

"So things quickly improved?"

"Oh . . ." That made it as simple as . . . everyone would obviously have it. "Perhaps in that one-to-one situation where he responded so readily to Mrs Johnson's humour, her personality, *yes* things did slowly pick up. But usually he was one in thirty and almost certainly felt the *odd* one in thirty and reacted to that threat."

"In what way?" pushed Mr Grey.

"Well in the classroom situation he was so terrified of failure, of being made to look a fool, that sort of thing, that he adopted all sorts of techniques to avoid doing the work, answering the question – or whatever it was he thought might show him up."

"What sort of techniques?"

"Oh, losing his pen, book – anything!" But I wasn't going to get away with that. "I'm afraid at his most outrageous he'd yell *fire,* pretend to slit his throat then fall to the floor."

Delinquent! I recognized that instinctive wince, half appalled, half disbelieving. "It was totally out of character," I rushed on to explain, "Mrs Johnson helped there too, acting as an inter-mediary."

"And he did this so as not to appear a fool!" said Mr Grey, incomprehension clear on his face. And I tried to say something about paradoxes and deep-seated anxieties and the worst case of self-failure that Mrs Johnson had ever known.

"The *worst* case?"

"Yes."

"She actually said that?"

"Yes."

"So why do you suppose that was?"

"Well . . ."

"Well?"

"Well . . ."

"How about the failure at the last school, the bullying, ridicule, disability?" put in the judge, as I again failed to answer.

"Fairly common I would have thought Your Honour, amongst the children in Mrs Johnson's care."

"I see-e-e . . . meaning?"

"Meaning that to understand this *worst* case we perhaps have to look further."

"Further than the school?" said the judge looking around the court as if he might find the answer there.

"Yes," said Mr Grey, "Mrs Roberts?"

* * *

And certain questions *do* have to be asked. And parents do ask them, Dear Psychiatrist, all the time. Perhaps if we had . . . ? Could it even be . . . ? If only . . . However, at least we didn't have any sort of marriage problem to aggravate . . . Though perhaps if we had, if saucepans had flown, it would have taken the accent away from him! *So the accent was on him?* Well yes, but we had quite a bit of the slit-throat syndrome ourselves, prompting us to ask more questions. And I'm sure you know how it goes on, Dear Psychiatrist, and on in a continuous round-and-round-the-mulberry-bush fashion until you turn psychiatrist yourself and say 'This soul-searching might be good up to a point, but it is very guilt-inducing and negative. Maybe it would be better to think *I have done my best!*'

But is that best good, good average, or just good for me . . . us . . .

* * *

"We had to let him see that we failed too," (yes, we should have been good at that) "and we had to persuade Giles to tone down talk that seemed founded on scores, averages and percentages – which Tom in fact loved but which Mrs Johnson felt was a chief cause of his wishing to win so much."

"And how about the *too-high parental expectations* which were a chief cause of his failing so much?" asked Mr Grey smartly and in another clear reference to The Heights Report, "Paragraph six lines 1-5," he added to guide the judge to this, "very telling criticism indeed!"

Which had sprung directly from an earlier – and even more telling – report, written after our first visit to The Heights, signed, sealed and circulated to all who had an interest in the fourteen year old Tom, excepting ourselves who only came to see it (almost by chance) some one and a half years later and *after* the court hearing, I explained.

"So that quite obviously it cannot be discussed yet, pivotal though it would seem to be!" pronounced the judge. And with the further advice to put the strong possibility of adverse parental pressure on hold until such time as it could be properly reviewed, the reasons behind the profound self-failure were, for the moment, dropped as the questioning moved to successes. "He gave up French," I said, "and the time thus gained . . ."

But just how to convey the gains that came to Tom by way of Mrs Johnson's humour, dynamism and wide-ranging talents? and to myself by her constant concern to keep me informed and involved . . . 'I've taken him out of maths since he *insists* he's rubbish. When I've built up his confidence (he has the infuriating habit of doing fractions in his head) I'll return him to the mainstream, but *not* to the bottom set' . . . 'I'm wondering what he understands about his tremor. We're very open about such things in the unit and Wayne asked him *why he shook so*. But I could see that it threw him – maybe a simple explanation from your GP would help?'[11] . . . *and* physiotherapy to improve stature and coordination (though called physical training, with emphasis on fitness – which is perhaps how he was persuaded to do horse riding too). *And* role play to help him cope better with social situations. *And* lessons on a typewriter for the old problem, *problem?* The old difficulty of thoughts racing ahead of ability to get them down . . .

Or across. *Must* emphasize second year geography expedition to the Lake District where he surprised everyone by his independence and industry. "Oh, and he climbed another mountain!" And so to the end of year exams which could also be cast in climbing terms.

"And did he think the results good, good average, or just good for him?" asked the judge.

"Well the outstanding one, the second in the class for chemistry, he went to enormous pains to explain to everyone that it was because he'd been given extra coaching. So I suppose he wasn't quite believing in himself. But at least he didn't yell fire or fall down dead any more!"

"Meaning he no longer feared appearing a fool?"

"Oh the fear was still there, but he was prepared to take risks. And the fear was significantly reduced because he was beginning to realize that not every encounter need necessarily be threatening or humiliating. But perhaps most important of all, Mrs Johnson got him laughing again, and gave us some rare glimpses of the old inimitable Tom."

"And how about home?" enquired Mr Grey.

"Oh no, I'm afraid he didn't laugh much there."

"What I mean is were things *generally* happier?"

"Well certainly the fact that I could ring Mrs Johnson any time made the situation much better."

"But otherwise the big improvement at school did not carry over?"

"Not really, no."

"But Mrs Roberts, you were only asked to let him see you failed!"

"I know, but he wouldn't believe us."

"So you failed!"

The judge nodded agreement while Mr Grey went on talking about *what should have happened because.* "Objection Your Honour, I would suggest my Learned Friend's line to be very simplistic, even blinkered."

"It seems clear to me," said the judge, looking all around the court as if to advertise the breadth of his vision, "that Mrs Johnson had an extraordinary talent. Whether, however, Mrs Roberts can actually be blamed for not sharing that talent is debatable, and perhaps for the jury alone to decide." And here the judge looked long and hard at the jury as if to impress upon them the weight of their task. "What we can all hope," he then continued, "is that as time went on, Mrs Johnson's good influence spilled over . . ."

"Oh no, well that's certainly what we hoped, but towards the end of Tom's first year at that school we heard Mrs Johnson was leaving. Well supposedly it was a year's leave of absence, but she in fact never went back – so it was the same thing. Except that all through the next year Tom lived in hopes of her return, as of course we did."

"Suggesting that you relied too heavily upon her!" said Mr Grey, stabbing with his finger on the notes he had made, no doubt of her talents.

"Oh we did try . . . what I mean is we did try very hard to carry on, to find the hobby he could be good at, or at least enjoy. Oh, there was another holiday *just with Dad*, that was a great success. But he wouldn't do horse riding from home, neither could we revitalize his interest in birds, in chess, *anything* . . ."

* * *

He even had to be persuaded to join family outings, Dear Psychiatrist, though we always chose to do something which we hoped would be of particular interest to Tom. Did this mean that such outings were more threatening than climbing a mountain *just with Dad* – and usually with Giles, his hero, as well? Perhaps suggesting that Jill was the threat? Jill was younger than Tom so that he seemed to find it necessary (as he had done since he was five) to prove himself better, more especially as she was a girl. Giles was older so should be better and consequently there was less pressure. Was that quite right? 'Giles is brilliant at everything, I'm rubbish!' And it was very difficult to address that cry from the heart to Tom's satisfaction. Certainly we could get Giles to tone down his talk on scores and averages – but we could hardly ask him to turn down his popularity or general success. Perhaps it helped that he wasn't around a great deal these days, being in constant demand for one school team or another.

So at least it might have been easier to do things *just with Dad* (or even with myself), particularly if he had been interested to do activities with considerably less appeal than was climbing a mountain.

'A walk Tom, to spot birds?'
'I'm not interested in that any more.'
Of course not, boring.
'Cooking?'
'No.'
Probably the wrong image.
'Television?'
'There's nothing on.'
Until the Saturday late night horror. Could that be dangerous

for a child so turned in on himself? Certainly I'd make no move to discourage such viewing since it's about all he'd do . . .

'Football – me in goal?'

'It depends!'

. . . on whether anyone's around who might look, laugh, snigger.

The game's good fun for three minutes – then a man appears the far side of the field, 'He's throwing sticks for his dog Tom – he's not the least bit interested in us!' But Tom dribbles inconsequentially till the man and the dog pass by, which is exasperating – if understandable. And odd. 'I feel a right Charlie standing here in the goal-mouth watching you dribble Tom!' And I know precisely why people watch you, and why people watching you makes you so watchful, and stiff, awkward, reluctant to venture out (which has something also to do with the fact that your school is such a long distance from home that you feel cut off, alienated).

'Slam it home Tom, he's gone now –

                   he'd have been quite impressed at that goal!'

'It was easy!'

'You mean I'm a lousy goal!'

A rare smile.

Progress.

Except that he's dribbling again. All the way home. For these boys who have just arrived are serious footballers, who certainly must not be allowed to see that Tom was reduced to playing with his mother. Furthermore they might stay two hours.

And for two hours he will be bored, pick arguments, harass the cat, raid the biscuit tin. 'A game of *anything* Tom?'

'No.'

Of course not. Possible to lose.

So some completely non-threatening pursuit that will capture his imagination, give purpose, stature, occupation. *Please!*

Once upon a time a handful of soldiers, a floor, some compelling facts and he was away – Wolfe storming Ontario, Richard Lionhart at the Gates of Jerusalem.

Or his own imaginative mixture of the two.

For his ninth birthday he'd wanted to go to a Civil War.[12] But there were no Civil Wars on just then so he'd settled for football.

Then there had been that afternoon when I'd wanted to watch the funeral of Field Marshall Montgomery.

A little cajoling first, for the pastoral scenes of the Field Marshall's native Hampshire were no match for the western showing on ITV. Suddenly a switch to Windsor where a sizable portion of Her Majesty's armed forces made Sitting Bull and his outfit look like a Sunday afternoon at the local gymkhana. 'Cor Mum, just look at all them millions of soldiers! I wish someone would give the order to start shooting!' A burst of vocal gunfire served until the cortege came into view, 'It's jolly silly to put a sword on the coffin isn't it Giles because Montgomery didn't fight with a sword! Is he dressed in his army stuff Mum? There must be millions and millions of soldiers there Giles – not many of them could have got killed at El Alamein!' – 'Don't be stupid Tom, that was years ago – these are modern soldiers!' – 'Well in that case Dad should be there!' – 'Dad was a Corporal in the army – that was before he became a Field Marshall!' – 'I know'.

Tom was just eight at the time.

* * *

"Now he is thirteen, Mrs Johnson has gone and we have heard . . ."

How the full extent of Tom's loss became daily more apparent in looks, intimations and sometimes in open speech, 'I don't want to go to that school if Mrs Johnson doesn't come back,' and, 'I don't like Mr Quixley!' And will he like you if being subjected to throat-slitting trials?

"And why, if Mrs Roberts proclaims herself to have been so uneasy, was it Mr Quixley – Mrs Johnson's replacement – who made the initial phone call regarding what he considered to be a worrying change in behaviour?"

Not working so hard.

Not wearing school tie.

Not wanting to go on school outing.

So *not* throat-slitting! Just three relatively minor nots, and Mr Quixley *not* ogre, might even be able to offer valuable new insights . . .

"So Mrs Roberts was eventually persuaded to be rather more positive herself – at least in adding to the overall picture."

'At home he is negative too, and has been ever since he began seeing himself as a failure – so that it is not a new problem, but long-term and a quite definite strategy to cope with . . .' Had I mentioned Learned Helplessness?[13] Probably not, but Mr Quixley *must* have recognized the syndrome from the tell-tale refusals and avoidances and which all added up to there being . . . 'Nothing that Tom can satisfactorily do, the need to succeed ruling out anything the least bit competitive and his poor coordination making him shy away from physical pursuits, so that time . . .'

". . . hangs on Mr Quixley's reply which was to render Mrs Roberts speechless – a singularly inappropriate response I would have thought since the clear intention had been to initiate, through the *active* involvement of the parent, a constructive and meaningful hobby for Tom. So that bearing also in mind the parental inadequacy which lies at the heart of this case, we must obviously look quite closely at this particular exchange, beginning with Mr Quixley's suggestion, given, I would remind you all, in response to Mrs Roberts' plea that *Tom be found something useful to do.* And I quote, 'If you could help him to build a canoe he could join a canoe club!'"

The tone was exactly right, straightforward, crisp, common-sense. What could possibly be more agreeable and appropriate? Except that . . . and that . . . and that . . . Didn't he have any idea? Obviously not – most likely one of the no-stuff-and-nonsense brigade, so how to answer?

"If you could help him to build a canoe," repeated Mr Grey, more buoyed up than before, "he could join a canoe club. A challenge," he went straight on, "very much in the spirit of *teach him to climb a mountain* I would have thought – however, Mrs Roberts seems this time to have reacted somewhat differently".

So what was the difference? Well the mountain needed a father, a free day, two good feet, determination, stamina – no particular problem. And the boat? A father again, many free days, fingers *and* thumbs. And didn't one also require rather specialist knowledge, expertise and equipment to build a canoe? Or were there now neat do-it-yourself packs suitable for a handyman with his saw and a bottle of glue? (just so long as he also has a degree in Chinese and a free weekend, preferably two). But this handyman had further to mastermind the meaningful involvement of an all-fingered and easily discouraged mate; that is to involve him in such a way that he will not feel all-fingered (failure here will cause immediate discouragement), but which is not so humdrum mundane as to dampen morale with the efficiency of water washing the wreck of a wet weekend. But of course the terrible fear of going under water, that was the only explanation necessary – to Mr Quixley then, and to Mr Grey now, together with Mr Quixley's, 'Well he'll just have to get over it than won't he!' And the firm put down of the receiver.

"It *is* quite possible to master fears!" said Mr Grey with a suitably curt and ice-cold detachment.

"Yes I know, and we did try very hard to help him to. But I think what really bothered me was that someone in charge of . . . well any child, but particularly of those with special difficulties, should have thought it such an easy thing to just *get over* a fear."

And Mr Grey seemed to agree whilst still finding it an easy thing to just *keep up* his attack. *No* I hadn't pursued that particular line with Mr Quixley. However, the next time that I'd gone in to school I had made it my business to introduce myself to him. This had happened to be as we were passing through some swing doors, and we'd stayed there, blocking half the doorway as the crowd continued to push past on the other side. "It was a social evening, a Christmas Fair I think. All that's quite irrelevant of course – it just sticks in my mind as contributing to the extreme discomfort."

"By which, we must take it, you were not hearing anything very complimentary!"

"No!" . . . and a lot more worrying than Tom's not wearing school tie – a tirade, relentless as the crashing door and the pushing crowds. "However, though I didn't really have any reason to question what he said, it did all seem very hard-hitting."

"You told him?"

"Not just like that but I did . . . well I apologized first for all the trouble that Tom was obviously being to the staff who were having to cope, but then I did try to say something about his *special* circumstances. However, the difficulty was that Mr Quixley said he had children in the unit with far, far greater handicaps than Tom *and they had decided to win!*"

"And you retorted?" said Mr Grey as pat as the thwack of the swing door, while Mr Quixley had been hot in pursuit of his next complaint. Yes perhaps I should have stopped him – for who can compare handicaps anyway? Certainly *he* had training in these things – so why didn't he realize that it can even be a handicap for a handicapped child to look able (as Tom fortunately did) so that no, or insufficient, allowances were made? And yes, why hadn't I told him that Tom *did* want to win? Wasn't that just another handicap, that he wanted to win so much? Or perhaps that he had been told too often that he couldn't!

"Speak up Mrs Roberts, so that the jury can hear!"

"But in the situation I was in . . . it just seemed there was nothing I could say without making things twenty times worse."

"So you said nothing?"

"Oh, I did ask why lessons on the typewriter had been stopped – you remember . . ."

"Yes, yes – thoughts in advance of what he could get down."

"Yes, well Mr Quixley explained that a typewriter was a valuable piece of equipment which would, however, only print what was fed into it."

"So Tom didn't have a thought in his head worth putting down?"

"No."

"You agreed?"

"No."

"You disagreed?"

"Not really."

"I see. I'd have thought Tom might have had one or two thoughts about Mr Quixley for a start! And what about the imagination? Once . . ."

. . . upon a time thoughts flew. Didn't say so, no, to invite scorn harder than the door. For *he* was the one nuisanced, lumbered, but only for a year. "My one idea was to appear reasonable, concerned – to try to keep things going until Mrs Johnson returned."

"Which, if this was a Christmas party, we can assume was two, three terms away?"

"Yes-s-s . . . two."

"How long were you in the swing doors with Mr Quixley Mrs Roberts, twenty minutes, half an hour perhaps?"

"I object Your Honour. Surely my Learned Friend can see how delicate this situation was? And short of the confrontational approach (which might come quite naturally to my Learned Friend) the mediatory role would seem . . ."

"Oh I do apologize Mrs Roberts – quite clearly you would have . . ."

Mr Quixley had apologized too – hoped that I understood the tough line he was taking, 'Well yes, it is *occasionally* effective, and what one is really aiming at is self-discipline . . .' – 'Oh he's miles away from that! It's extremely doubtful he'll achieve it at this school. He's a loner identifying with the unruly element of whatever age group.'

"And the outcome Mrs Roberts?"

"Oh, Mr Quixley finished by saying that Tom needed to go through childhood again."

"You were able to arrange for that were you Mrs Roberts?"

But the reality wasn't funny and hadn't seemed much easier – three weeks of *coping the best we could* and all the time dreading the Head Master might ring and say they couldn't manage any longer (and who would have him then – maladjusted?). Then another journey to school, I wasn't summoned no, just a regular evening to receive subject reports from the house tutor in the main part of the school. But no less worrying for that, and absolutely imperative that I should go, crawling on knees if necessary to apologize, if only words would come . . .

"Speak up Mrs Roberts – so that the jury can hear!"

"Yes – Miss Amey, the house tutor, got in first to say that Tom was a quiet, nervous boy, all his subject reports being quite good, particularly physics and biology."

"Could you repeat that please Mrs Roberts?"

Most sat in stupefied silence, as I had, while the judge, who had spoken, waited pen in hand to write down the report once it had been fully promoted again. "And you told the house tutor of Mr Quixley's words?" he then said.

"Just a little – to explain my stunned reaction. And that brought fresh protestations of his good behaviour. Miss Amey said that she never had any trouble at all. She had noticed that some boys *got at him* – but he coped with this well."

"GOT AT HIM, GOT AT HIM!" thundered Mr Grey, *"Had noticed!* Had she done nothing about it? – No? Because he coped with it well? So what did *you* do? Speak up Mrs Roberts, so that the jury can hear!"

But I couldn't . . . just couldn't explain I'd felt proud, even elated at such control, after the worry of the last report. "I asked if he had any friends."

"Just like that? The house tutor reports that boys *got at him* and all you do is ask if he has any friends?"

"Objection Your Honour, in such a plight of course . . ."

. . . he would want a friend, even one who might well have added to his problems. But the details could be given in terms of glowing pride and soaring elation, and more or less as they were to me then. 'He does have one, a notorious trouble-maker called Gary – so if he's good in his company then he *must* be well-behaved!'

"That was the house tutor's reckoning was it?"

"Yes." And perhaps useful illumination might have been afforded by Mrs Johnson's earlier view, 'I am encouraging the friendship as in some ways they compliment each other well, Tom is better academically but Gary is tougher.'

"You didn't think to question anything?"

"No . . . however, once I got home, I questioned Tom. I asked why I'd had two such totally different reports in the space of three weeks."

"And?"

"His exact words were, 'Well Mum, Mr Quixley is a very difficult man to get on with!'"

"Which took you to Mr Quixley?"

"Oh . . . no."

"Of course not, Mr Quixley was a very difficult man to get on with wasn't he Mrs Roberts!"

There was no disputing that. Cold. Blunt. Hard as the door slamming to.

A few weeks later still a Mrs Anderson, second in command at the unit, contacted me with yet a third report, welcome, helpful, eminently quotable.

"Yet you do insist," interrupted the judge, "that she did not necessarily contradict anything that Mr Quixley had said, it was her *interpretation* that was different?"

"Wide open, enlightened," supplied Mr Shore, "versus hard, dour?"

"I think perhaps we should have some *concrete* examples Mr Shore – If Mrs Roberts could oblige?"

"Yes, well of course I rang Mr Quixley two or three weeks after receiving his complaints to ask if there had been any improvement. He replied, 'Yes he is doing work, but only because he knows that he has to, so that it's being done in a mechanical and truculent manner'. This might perhaps be compared to Mrs Anderson's worry that *Tom had reached a plateau and needed some fresh impetus*. She eventually worked out what that impetus might be, and successfully challenged him in a new direction. Then again, what Mrs Anderson saw as, 'Perfectly understandable behaviour in the face of seemingly overwhelming odds,' Mr Quixley read as, 'Stemming from an intrinsic personality problem,' and further to this what he pronounced 'sadistic' she considered to be, 'Coping in the only way he knew how,' and that was the use of his tongue to wound the one or two he could find to be weaker than himself . . . I'm afraid this happens."

"Don't apologize Mrs Roberts," Mr Grey consoled, "maybe it was a good thing that he *could* sometimes stand up for himself – perhaps that's what he could be good at!"

"But . . ."

* * *

That's what worried me almost to distraction, Dear Psychiatrist, that Tom would become a bully, hard, malicious – allow Mr Quixley the last laugh.

Tom laughed hardly at all now, and talked less, actually resented being spoken to – especially if there was a third person present making him the odd one . . . making him *feel* the odd one, in spite of everything you did . . . *because* of everything you did to try and help. Whether there was a third person there or not.

But at least he could let go at home, and sometimes did. Though most of the time he paced the room like a caged animal. From Miss Amey there was, at the end of the school year, one further report that he was, 'too quiet, impossible to get to know'. But Mrs Anderson was worried – chiefly because his tremor was so much worse. Yes it was known that he was called names, (all prefixed by *shaking*) and yes attempts were being made to stop this, or to get him not to mind so much.

But the tremor got worse – which led to more ridicule.

* * *

"So to sum up," said Mr Grey with a decision that meant to reduce to convenient terms a somewhat protracted episode, "the tremor got worse, Mrs Roberts felt as a result of the ridicule.

However, the small chance of its being something more serious, such as a progressive disease or a brain tumour, got him referred to a neurologist. The neurologist, it was subsequently to emerge, had been very irritated by the letter of referral in which the particulars were, shall we just say, *fully* detailed (though exactly whom this letter was from has yet to be established). Tom, on the other hand, had been briefed scarcely at all as to why it had been thought necessary he should see a neurologist," (hard look at me tells everyone precisely whom quarrel is with here) "tremor being a *taboo* word!"

"Does my Learned Friend not realize . . ."

That he has hit a very sensitive area. For tremor, to Tom, equalled ridicule, failure and a rampaging anxiety which yes, had made my explanations as to the reasons for this visit very brief, almost of the 'doctor will know what to do' variety.

"Perhaps *my* Learned Friend will, however, concede that Mrs Roberts' hope that the word *tremor* should not come up during a consultation arranged specifically to discuss a *tremor* did rather hang on the neurologist's agreeing to use telepathy, or perhaps . . ."

On his calling me in ahead of Tom for the discussion of issues which the letter of referral would have made abundantly clear were very painful to Tom. Or just on his being decently sensitive. 'Tom Roberts, where's Tom Roberts? TOM ROBERTS – COME ON, COME ON AND BRING YOUR MOTHER TOO!' Did he have to stare Tom up and down as if a weird neurological specimen? He was angry! That's what I'd failed to convey, the hostility, so intense, so brutal that it would have been little easier if I had discussed with Tom the *taboo tremor* from the first firmly crossed T's to each and every dotted I of the insensitivities that might come by the way of it.

'I see you're very worried about the worsening tremor' – 'Not really worried but . . .' – 'WELL IS IT WORSE OR ISN'T IT?'

'What else is worse?'

'What's he like at school?'

'What's his writing like?'

'What's he like at sports?'

'What's his run like?'

"Perhaps my Learned Friend would like to tell Mrs Roberts how she might have prepared her son for such messages as might be conveyed by the question, 'Are his brother and sister a lot better than he is?' Remembering too that these questions were being brusquely put to further convey . . ."

Perhaps I *should* have asked for Tom to go out, yes. However, once he'd got the gist of what was being said, surely he'd have worried more then about what was being said behind his back?

"So you answered all those questions in front of him?"

"Yes, but wrapping them up so carefully I hoped Tom wouldn't follow. Then the doctor got angry thinking I was being evasive, uncooperative and . . . well stupid really. But once Tom was out of earshot getting ready for an examination, I could at least *attempt* to set the record straight."

'I see you're worried about the tremor and various other things you don't wish to discuss with me!' – 'No it's really not like that, it's just that there are certain things I couldn't possibly say while Tom was here . . .' – 'What *I* want to know is whether anything other than the tremor has got worse?' – 'Certainly the behaviour . . .' – 'I'M NOT INTERESTED IN ALL THAT!' And a finger flipping the referral letter pointed to another source of friction. 'I really can't think what you're making so much fuss about since the tremor's the only thing that's worse – what did you expect me to do for you?'

"Mr Shore," said the judge, interrupting a point Mr Shore was trying to put, "since Tom was out of the room getting ready for an examination at the time you are referring to, I think we need not labour too much the abuse aimed specifically at Mrs Roberts. What we do, however, need to do is to establish whether the result of that examination *did* confirm the neurologist right in his opinion that Mrs Roberts was stupid in considering such a remote possibility as a brain tumour, when the tremor (given that worries concerning the behaviour didn't count) was the only thing that was worse?"

"Yes it did," I said stupidly, thus similarly branding the doctor who had referred us, two or three teachers and Bill. "But please

could I just say in my defence, that there were other things that
might have been worse, his handwriting, coordination, speech,
(I even had fears concerning his personality) – it's just that I
hadn't felt quite able to be honest in the answers that I gave,
because of Tom being there and not wishing to damage his
confidence even further than . . ."

"You hadn't spoken the truth!" And the judge's tone clearly
carried the reverberation *'In this place where one must also speak
the truth, the whole truth, and nothing but the truth'*. "So could
you even hope for an accurate diagnosis? What did you expect
the neurologist might do for you?" he asked in much the same
exasperated way the neurologist had used to ask this question
himself.

'If you like I can do a skull X ray and EEG.' – 'No, I've
really no wish for these tests to be done on my account as it
were.' "It was alright because there was a second doctor present,
she hadn't really spoken before but now said, very firmly, that
Tom *must* have an EEG and also a brain scan rather than the
skull X-ray that Dr Heavens had suggested – and those tests
would provide confirmation, one way or the other, if you see
what I mean."

"Dr Heavens being the name of the neurologist?" said the
judge, taking up The Heights Report.

"Yes, that's right."

And now Mr Grey and Mr Shore looked at their copies too
to read how, 'Dr Heavens had been extremely kind in spending
so much time talking over the case with the parents'. And the
jury awaited enlightenment.

"If we miss out *extreme kindness*," said Mr Grey with one
eye on his Learned Friend who seemed poised to object, "Can
we at least take it that Dr Heavens spent time in talking the case
over with you Mrs Roberts?"

"On the second occasion when I took my husband along for
moral support, he did, yes. It was the first time, when Tom was
actually there, that he was so irritable, even *before* the
consultation had really begun – I think the letter of referral . . ."

The judge, Mr Grey and Mr Shore all made to speak together,

the counsels giving way to the judge, "Which doctor was it who referred you Mrs Roberts?"

"Dr Farnstrom, a psychiatrist from The Heights Unit for Adolescents."

"The Heights – we haven't even got there yet!"

"No, I'm sorry, I've taken things in the wrong order."

"Then I'm afraid I have absolutely no alternative," said the judge sternly, "but to declare everything that you have just reported as totally *out of order*." The court was ordered to forget everything that had been said on the subject and the jury looked immensely relieved.

Tom had not been so lucky. 'I didn't like him much Mum, but I suppose he was only doing his job.'

* * *

And when we started to have the tests done, Dear Psychiatrist, there were further complications, some unavoidable, others not. For instance the tubes containing the blood samples got broken so that we had to return for a second test. The brain scan and the EEG were to have been done on the same day, but the EEG had to be postponed because The Fairlands Psychiatric Unit for Young Children refused to release the records of the one they'd had done when Tom was six. So there was a long delay over that, we eventually having to return for a third, or was it a fourth time when, presumably, The Fairlands Unit had had a change of mind. The secretary to the Neurological Department was furious, mentioned (quite spontaneously) *interdepartmental in-fighting* and further volunteered, 'You just wouldn't believe what goes on here!'

However, the tests were conducted very kindly and, in time, we heard they were all completely normal (this time the meeting with Dr Heavens being quite friendly). So, Dear Psychiatrist, in the absence of pathological reasons for the worsening tremor, the possibility that bullying and ridicule were responsible didn't seem an unreasonable hypothesis – though I do realize I must be careful. And I did always try to be honest, one part of me thinking 'he has a tremor; the tremor is (probably) being made worse by ridicule; this is compounding the failure that he has felt himself to be ever since he has been capable of evaluating his performance against others' (the tremor – highlighted by ridicule – being an integral part of that evaluation). And if I can accept this I can think, 'when he leaves school and the bullying and the ridicule stop (though of course it might not) things *should* improve'. However, another part of me thinks, 'though his predicament is quite clear, given that there are at least three teachers at his school who bend over backwards to help (and Mr Quixley has now gone), is the amount of anger and frustration he shows quite justified? . . . which leads me to wonder if the anger and the hostility have become part of him'. Though I don't wonder quite calmly like that, for my anxiety now is as much a nightmare as his rather different nightmare. He only communicates to start an argument, paces the room, breaks things (that's part of the worsening tremor), raids the biscuit tin and lives for Saturday and his machines. Oh – he's discovered one-armed bandits and the like, and it's amazing how little trouble his problems are when competing against a machine . . . so perhaps when peer-pressure is removed on leaving school there is a chance of success in some totally non-threatening occupation?

On leaving school he will enter the open competition of the job market at a time of probable high unemployment and where there will be no statutory obligation – as at school – to accommodate the poorly-coordinated-low-morale-no-hope-written-all-over-face-the-facts-now-and-institute-some-change.

I *will* help. But spend all my time attempting to eliminate potential flash-points, picking up the pieces, contriving peace, cool tempers, a warm welcome home from school – which is wrong (as is every other type of greeting right through to no welcome at all – which is also wrong). 'Why do you cheer up so much when Giles and Dad come home?' he then throws at me.

Should I have told him? Perhaps given some insight into the

gloom-spreading potency of his behaviour? Once upon a time this might have been achieved through a joke. Jokes nowadays misfired, along with every other attempt to inject some fun into his life. But at least he can look forward to his Saturday trips. (As *we* can look forward to the hours he is away. *What if Giles and Jill say life is better without him?* But they don't and I DON'T LET MYSELF think about the dangers of such a vulnerable child alone in Amusement Arcadia.) And the fact that he needs to finance the trips does motivate him towards further valuable occupation – chiefly washing-up type jobs – which he does with some satisfaction (particularly at his father's work-place). We ignore the breakages . . . but worry a lot about who would employ anyone so slow, so disorganized, so morose. 'Have you any idea what you might do when you leave school Tom?' – 'No' – 'Perhaps you could . . . ?' – 'I'd be useless' – 'You don't know till you've tried!' – 'I do I'd be useless' – 'I think you'd manage' – 'You're just saying that!' – 'No I do think . . .' I long for the inspired utterance of a Mrs Johnson (at least he might have seen I failed, and so completely as to share all the complexes of the useless-syndrome). And I go into school every time there is one of those evenings to discuss *progress, the future.* What could be better than that he should leave school with one or two qualifications (what if he fails?). We'd been told several times that he should be capable of CSE maths (and science and art) so that I *drive* myself across on the appropriate evening to get his name down.

And immediately wonder *what am I doing* amongst such confident, normal parents who stand around amiably chatting, knowing good prospects, each other and no great urgency to leave. But I must go through with it now, like entering an exam myself, in which presentation would be the all-important factor.

The maths master was appalled. 'You've come about Tom Roberts? *Tom Roberts!* I just can't believe it – you really mean you've come about Tom Roberts? Absolutely hopeless! Do you know he's with children who can't add two and two together and who can't spell their names? To tell you the truth Mrs Roberts I've no patience with this *special unit-business* – we get them from everywhere!' I remember so well the words, the tone, exasperation, incredulity, acute discomfort. Mr Crompton had stepped back as if startled by my initial enquiry, and remained at that uneasy distance throughout the entire length of his tirade. And yes he did examine me, hard – as if he couldn't really believe I was all there, such stupidity, such complete want of understanding.

* * *

"So are we perhaps to put two and two together ourselves Mrs Roberts, to try and work out what it was that this master said – on exam chances, future prospects maybe?"

"Yes, perhaps both since he told me that Tom was no good at all, that he wouldn't work, that he was all bottled up and tense like an unexploded bomb. And then he added, 'To tell you the truth Mrs Roberts, I think he's the sort of boy who will get into trouble with the police one day!'"

"Perhaps Mrs Roberts we should just deal with the psychiatric period first!"

"Objection Your Honour! Is that my Learned Friend's way of suggesting that Mrs Roberts is fabricating? Or is he being frivolous? Either way . . ."

"I was merely thinking that as Mrs Roberts is unlikely to challenge this teacher – for reasons that we have gone into before – we might as well follow where things are obviously going."

"Then I think I would have to advise you Mr Grey," interrupted the judge, "that you are failing in your duty which, I might remind you, is to discover whether Mrs Roberts did everything in her power to ensure that her son developed as well as possible. Since the police have now been mentioned, I would have thought that several quite pertinent lines of enquiry might have occurred to you."

"Yes Your Honour," said Mr Grey with the merest of bows. "Well Mrs Roberts," he went on, "leaving aside the police for one moment, perhaps we should just establish whether you did challenge this master over anything?"

"Well yes, I did mention that Tom had scored 78% and 98% in the previous year's maths exams, and though I appreciated they might have been easy papers, the teacher he'd had then did say he should be entered for CSE maths. But Mr Crompton fairly exploded at that, telling me it was, 'No easy option – they have to do decimals and fractions!'"

"Which no doubt prompted you to mention his practice of doing fractions in his head? And to enquire as to why such a boy should be with children who cannot add two and two together?" Mr Grey concluded.

"Objection Your Honour! I would suggest that if my Learned Friend were himself to put two and two together, he might quite quickly see that this master is another very difficult man to get on with and that Mrs Roberts, as the parent of a boy perceived as a trouble-maker (even if only at the unexploded-bomb stage) is going to feel her position extremely weak. If my Learned Friend would then like to put three and three together, or perhaps, and even more appropriately, to take everything away from the answer he gets, he might just realize that – by this stage – Mrs Roberts' spirits were in all probability too low to do any challenging."

"Mr Shore I hardly think that low spirits can be accepted as sufficient reason for failing to take appropriate action," said the judge who then, by the slightest movement of his head, indicated that Mr Grey should continue his challenging.

"Perhaps Mrs Roberts," Mr Grey continued, "it would be appropriate to discover whether you were indeed in low spirits at this stage?"

"Yes I was."

"And was this because of the state of the maths or because you had been advised that Tom might be in trouble with the police one day?"

"Mr Grey, it's not *why* Mrs Roberts was in low spirits that needs to be investigated so much as whether it affected the way that she managed her son, particularly at this stage when she has just been told he is a hopeless case and might be in trouble with the police one day."

"Yes Your Honour. Mrs Roberts, did your low spirits affect the way that you managed your son?"

"Not regarding the maths no, because the day after my talk with the maths master he sent me a message to say that he'd entered Tom for the exam. So I decided to start coaching him myself."

"Tom being the pawn in this contest?"

"Does my Learned Friend really think . . ."

'Mr Crompton says to tell you he's put my name down for that exam.' – 'Oh, well I'll help you if you like.' A low-key opening gambit and the game (largely using football-based questions) was joined quite willingly, and with a slow, steady advance, one step at a time. There developed too a reasonable understanding of *all* the principles involved so that eventual success could be a very real hope (as with science and art) pawn through to checkmate(s).

However I have got things in the wrong order again, for these pluses belong to the sixteen year old school leaver just-beginning-to-find-his-feet stage, whereas we should still be at fourteen-everything-going-to-pieces . . .

* * *

Dear Psychiatrist,

Tom was in fact fourteen and a couple of months, when Mrs Anderson got in touch regarding the worsening tremor and various other problems on which she felt she needed guidance. She asked if we would agree to Tom seeing an educational psychologist and Mrs Masters was contacted. However, Mrs Masters advised that it was now *your* greater expertise that was required; advice that initially concerned me, feeling, as I did, that in-depth discussion might well add to Tom's problems. I was though finally persuaded that you were *enormously professional and very sensitive in dealing with these things.*

The referral was not quite straightforward for neither Mrs

Masters not Mrs Anderson had the power to arrange it. So Tom had another investigation to enable a school medical officer (who did have the power, but who had not seen Tom since he was three) to write the report necessary to the application. She was very nice, but obviously not able to supply that type of detail which will afford valuable insight. In fact she may have indicated quite incorrectly for she called him . . . though not to his face . . . a delinquent.

Was that necessarily wrong?

Yes! No . . . I don't know.

When Tom was three this doctor's 'Was he a forceps?' had given hard, but real definition to my long, private wranglings. Now three more years of agonizing seemed similarly certified by her, 'Don't worry, The Heights are extremely good, particularly with delinquents'.

So The Heights *was* the right destination.

Perhaps it would even be good to talk, and in a place where digressions were the norm.

Normally one kept quiet.

(There was no 'Family-with-a-Disturbed-Child Anonymous'; and for Tom's sake one did wish to be anonymous; so anonymous that one cut right down on social engagements in attempting to avoid potentially embarrassing situations; which was rather hard on Giles and Jill.)

But now we could talk where absolutely nothing need be held back from Miss Godden, psychiatric social worker – Tom meanwhile talked with Dr Farnstrom, psychiatrist. So beginning with the difficult early years we moved smartly to the exciting middle period when there were so many advances in every direction – reading, writing, chess playing, the first steps in social readiness . . .

* * *

"Mrs Roberts, I think we would all understand what is involved in the giving of a Case History – no doubt you also detailed the difficult later years, go on from there."

"Yes, but please could I first say that Miss Godden didn't actually believe me when I said that Tom once played chess, in fact I don't really think she believed anything I said about the good years four to nine."

"She challenged you?"

"No, that's the problem, she didn't. If only she had, things might have been *so* different. No, I was to discover her views in a report, which was in fact sent to all those who had an interest in the case, though I myself didn't come to see it until some twenty months after this point, when we'd completely finished at The Heights."

"So we'll come to that in time, go on from . . ."

"Objection Your Honour! Obviously such a gross error of judgement is going to have a serious effect on the way that this family is viewed!"

"Mr Shore, what we are trying to do is to recreate as closely as possible the conditions existing at the time. Please continue Mrs Roberts."

"Yes . . . then perhaps I ought to mention one other thing that happened *before* this meeting with Miss Godden, if we are taking things in their strict order, and that is that she had – as part of the usual preparation – read Tom's Case History including, of course, the early assessment and IQ by Mr Leroy and also Dr Heckman's findings."

"Just remind me Mrs Roberts, who was Dr Heckman?" asked the judge.

"Oh . . . he was the psychiatrist we met when Tom was six."

"Oh yes, of course, the one who talked about exhausted parents and nervous wrecks of children – or was it nervous wrecks of parents and exhausted . . ." The judge's voice trailed off as he looked back through his notes passing, "*Absolutely hopeless . . . poor self opinion . . . Cerebellar Ataxia . . . failure . . . determination to succeed . . . very handicapped . . . chess playing . . . there is absolutely nothing wrong with your child!* And what is someone new to the case to make of all that!"

he said, looking up with considerable puzzlement on his face, "Perhaps the only reasonable approach for such a person would be to keep an open mind," he finished judiciously.

"Which certainly Miss Godden did not!" Mr Shore quickly responded, "For she credited the obsolete IQ, rejected the chess playing, and, in the very next sentence, complained of *parents who had a very poor understanding of their son's limitations and who had consequently placed undue pressure . . .*"

"Mr Shore we don't know that yet! So please would you go on Mrs Roberts."

"Knight to queen's bishop three I think Mrs Roberts."

"Mr Shore, are you talking to Mrs Roberts in code?"

"No Your Honour – just a somewhat arbitrary way of saying *your move*. I could as easily have said pawn to king's knight four."

"Then kindly say what you have to say in plain English. Ambiguities can so easily lead to mistakes. Please continue Mrs Roberts."

"Yes, well to return to the Case History, I of course spent a great deal of time detailing the failure and the bullying, his overfamiliarity with both causing such a loss of self-esteem and confidence that he had virtually withdrawn . . ."

"Mrs Roberts I don't think we want all the details again, so shall we move on?"

"Yes – perhaps to the mistake concerning my husband . . ."

"Mrs Roberts," interrupted the judge, "You will please not announce it a mistake – that tends to lead to biased opinion".

"Oh sorry, yes. At some stage Miss Godden asked my husband how he and Tom got on together, and Bill said, in his usual self-effacing way, 'Oh poor old Tom, I expect all his problems are due to his father's not understanding him,' and that was obviously so ridiculous that I laughed . . ."

"*Obviously* ridiculous?"

"Well no, I suppose not, because Miss Godden took him literally, though it was only much later that we discovered that. At the time she asked no questions nor queried the statement in any way – so that more misunderstandings followed, though of course we weren't able to work out precisely what was amiss until we saw how she had quoted and very much heightened his words . . ."

"In The Heights Report which you didn't see until many months later at the trial! Return to the primary interview please."

"Yes – when the Case History was finished Miss Godden met privately with Dr Farnstrom for the exchanging of information – Dr Farnstrom, you will remember, had been talking with Tom. Then, after about half an hour we were called, together with Tom, to sit with them in what I imagine was supposed to be a relaxed circle, Dr Farnstrom opening the meeting by saying, 'What are your problems and how can we help you?'"

* * *

Dear Psychiatrist,
I don't know what Tom talked about during his meeting with Dr Farnstrom, though I could tell from his face – when we met mid-morning between sessions – that it had been a difficult experience, probably for both of them, for Tom did not enjoy talking about himself, even in a superficial way, and closed like a clam at anything deeper.

That is except with one very special person whom he went to once a week, ostensibly to play the guitar. In fact the sessions turned more and more to just *talking* – about matters superficial and then deep, as she very gradually won his confidence. Although we could not at that time achieve anything approaching this constructive relationship, we did try very hard to keep the lines of communication open (Bill could sometimes even make him laugh) and also to introduce him – before we came to see you – to the idea that people at The Heights would try to help through talking.

* * *

"Cases are not usually won by a state of speechlessness Mrs Roberts! If you remember, Dr Farnstrom asked, 'What are your problems and how can we help you?'"

"Does my Learned Friend not realize that the quickest way to lose the case was to answer that question – given the anxiety that Tom feels in discussing problems with one person, let alone a whole circle!"

"And does my Learned Friend not realize that Tom could not have been the first adolescent presenting at a psychiatric unit with acute anxiety and lack of confidence! These people are professionals and *must* use tried and tested methods."

But was this 'in at the deep end' the only approach? Leaving us frantically seeking escape . . .

"So we are to read are we Mrs Roberts that Dr Farnstrom's invitation was met by a stony silence?"

"Oh . . . we eventually thought to say that it was the school who had requested the visit."

"And how do you suppose that must have appeared to them?"

"Objection Your Honour! Has Mrs Roberts got to spell it all out? Obviously she, and Mr Roberts, would feel upset to have Tom placed in what would be a very testing position were the original question to be honestly answered. And the psychiatric team, if unable to perceive the real situation, would no doubt be writing labels – uncooperative, overprotective, resistant to help . . ."

"Mr Shore I don't think that we should put words into Mrs Roberts' mouth," advised the judge.

"Oh, but I think that's exactly what did happen, eventually anyway. More immediately Dr Farnstrom insisted that we *must* have problems too – as well as the school that is."

"So another silence?"

"Oh . . . Bill eventually thought to say that one of Tom's chief problems was that he had such a poor opinion of himself. That *seemed* alright because it implied that he was quite wrong in this opinion. But Dr Farnstrom said that Tom might have difficulties following such verbal leads and explanations – were we aware of this?"

"Implying you had a very poor understanding of your son?"
"Yes."
"A serious indictment in the context of this case which . . ."
"Objection . . ."
. . . no objection no, Too taken aback and anyway, *something* seemed unseemly. So our 'yes' was expedient, to head off talk on difficulties and limitations. While Tom sat hunched up, looking miserable, diminished. Thus no doubt furthering the *limited* label . . .
"And, are we to assume, another silence?"
"Yes. Then after a bit, Dr Farnstrom pushed for more problems."
"And?"
"I think that's when I decided to be quite honest. You see, we had grave reservations about taking Tom to a psychiatric unit. However, Mrs Masters had persuaded us that we should, just to make sure that Tom's difficulties were being investigated at a great enough depth (a depth which she, as a psychologist, felt unequal to) and treated with sufficient expertise. Therefore, once it seemed that treatment was going to be a case of talking things through, and in a way that I felt might add to Tom's problems, I asked, if they hadn't found anything untoward, would it please be possible to be referred back to Mrs Masters – as she knew him so well?"
"In other words," supplied Mr Grey, "we don't like what you're offering, we know someone better – can we go please . . . ?"

LIBRARY
SEVENOAKS HOSPITAL
HOSPITAL ROAD
SEVENOAKS
TN13 3PG

* * *

The gulf widened. But Bill was trying to put things right, 'We don't mean to be ungrateful but families are fairly resilient and learn to cope' – 'Yes, and we certainly have no wish to force ourselves on you, however, every member of the family is bound to be affected – would it help if we came to your house to meet Giles and Jill?' That got a reaction from Tom, 'No, I wouldn't like that at all!' They looked surprised – was that because they now realized that Tom *could* react? Or was it that other young people were much readier to fall in with that type of plan? They appeared to respect my concern that Tom would feel very threatened by such a visit and the next meeting was arranged to take place at Tom's school (so we weren't to be referred back to Mrs Masters, but they would keep her posted – she could even come to the meeting at the school). Did we have any questions? Tom did, 'You're not going to come to our house to meet Giles and Jill are you?' – 'Not this time, but it might be necessary one day!' We left then, with Tom still very agitated. 'They're not going to come to our house are they?' – 'No Tom!' – 'But what if they do?' – 'They can't unless we agree' – 'But what if they do?' – 'I've explained Tom they . . .' – 'But what if they do?'

* * *

Dear Dr Farnstrom,
I do apologize if we seemed uncooperative and unforthcoming at the meeting today.
We in fact had many concerns that we wished to discuss with you, however, we felt very reluctant to do so in front of Tom. Would it please be possible to meet again privately with you?

* * *

And Dr Farnstrom apologized too, at the meeting that was set up. He had, he said, only just read Dr Heckman's notes on the Fairlands' visit to see that we had clashed with people there, 'It must be very difficult for you to go through it all again'.

Not *clashed* no, and not with *people*. That stung like a slap in the face of which . . . don't overreact! Leaping defence will merely suggest confrontational type . . . but I must say something to put the record straight, in the measured tones of ONE WHO IS IN CONTROL.

* * *

"*One* who is in control?"

"Oh . . . at the meeting that I had with Dr Farnstrom and Miss Godden, it was . . ."

"*I* had?"

"Well Tom wasn't there – that was the point, I'd asked for a confidential meeting without Tom."

"And without your husband?"

"Not necessarily, but . . . well, to be honest, he didn't enjoy going to The Heights and I thought I could manage without him."

"I see! You don't think that might have suggested a certain lack of interest, solidarity, perhaps even hinted at a bad relationship between father and son?"

"Objection Your Honour! Short of Mrs Roberts being a mind reader she would have no way of knowing such feelings were abroad for . . ."

"Mr Shore, we cannot be sure of that yet! So let us return to the confidential talk, if Mrs Roberts is willing to divulge . . . ?"

"It's alright yes, and they were very sympathetic – though neither Dr Farnstrom nor Miss Godden reassured, or even commented on my chief worry . . ." . . . or was it my hope, 'When Tom leaves school and the bullying and the ridicule hopefully stop, do you think he might change back to the happy, thoughtful, enjoyable person he once was? Or is the anger, aggression, that sort of thing, now a fixed part of him . . . even worse, could it all stem from that forceps delivery, because, if so, couldn't it worsen?' "I wanted reassurance that certain worrying behavioural aspects were not set or likely to intensify, that they might perhaps lessen as conditions improved, might even seem immediately reduced if I could get some explanation, some word of hope . . . and when they said nothing I'm afraid . . ."

"Well obviously Mrs Roberts they would not be able to answer such a question lightly – they'd have to get to know him first."

'Yes but please *not* through the group therapy, he finds talking about his tremor, about being rubbish, the ridicule and everything so difficult even in the most relaxed circumstances, and when the focus is so on him' – 'But Mrs Roberts, he's got to face up to his handicap, even if it is painful!' Dr Farnstrom had insisted.

"Yes, I could see that the psychiatrist must probe a little, try to draw Tom out, and perhaps he did in their private talks. The trouble was the group meeting it was always insisted should follow, for it just seemed that talking things through with four – even three adults was the not the right way." Some understood, I could see. Others uncomprehending, remote as a jury who decide . . . "No, they never asked where Bill was, just said – to Tom and myself – what were our problems and how could they help? So eventually I began mentioning things that weren't really worrying, but which did allow the sort of participation that I thought was wanted – to give them the fuller picture that would help them to guide us, advise the school. Oh, and they pressed again, and again, and again about coming to our house to see Giles and Jill; they said they couldn't really help otherwise. . ."

* * *

Dear Psychiatrist,
After a quite enormous amount of pressure from Dr Farnstrom that he and Miss Godden should visit out house to meet Giles

and Jill, I finally rang Mrs Masters to get her advice. She was very concerned that we were finding the meetings so upsetting and that it was not you in charge of the case. She said that some of the young registrars were very keen on family therapy, but that it did not work for everyone. She did however feel that, if we could manage it, we should let the meeting with Giles and Jill go ahead for they might well have worries that they would like to express and 'The Heights' people were really very professional in dealing with these things'.

* * *

"So are we to take it Mrs Roberts that you agreed, but very grudgingly, to the home visit?"

"Oh . . . well perhaps reluctantly."

"And what interpretation do you suppose was . . ."

"Might I suggest Overprotective with a great womb-like 'O' . . ."

I don't know, I really don't know! 'You won't let them come will you Mum?' – 'They can't come unless we agree,' – 'It really would be so helpful,' – 'But Tom is very unhappy about such a visit!' – 'When can we come?' – 'But even Giles and Jill . . .' – 'Might have things they would like to say,' – 'But Tom . . .' – 'Will be more relaxed in his home – so we will get to know him better' – 'But I . . .' am standing in the way of . . .

"Order! Now perhaps we can hear what Mrs Roberts has to say."

"They did come yes, and no, it wasn't quite as stressful as I'd feared. Impossible to give any sort of analysis – each child was interviewed privately by either Dr Farnstrom or Miss Godden. And certainly I was grateful for all the time and trouble they were taking over the case – they'd been to the school too where the chief concerns were Tom's tension and his tremor. It was of course Dr Farnstrom who arranged for Tom to see the neurologist, you remember I took that in the wrong order."

"So that now things might be said to be in the right order as it were, perhaps you could tell the court what Dr Farnstrom advised, once he had collected information from the various visits and from the neurological investigations."

"Oh no, by the time the report from the neurologist had come through Dr Farnstrom had moved to another hospital. So the reassurance that I had hoped for, concerning Tom's behaviour, never came."

"Neither, presumably, did the gloomy prognosis you had feared?"

"No."

"You see Mrs Roberts, there are always two ways to view a thing!"

* * *

Right or wrong. Was I wrong Dear Psychiatrist, as I was always – through looks and intimations – made to feel? Certainly I was prompted to ask questions of myself, and also of Dr Farnstrom on our last meeting, 'Should we persuade Tom to talk about his tremor, sense of failure – things like that, given that he gets so upset, but also bearing in mind the fact that it would be possible to help him more if he could be persuaded to talk?' – 'Yes, but only do so in the most sensitive way. Be alert to signs of distress and respect his privacy on the matter'.

But wasn't that precisely what I'd been saying all along? And wasn't that precisely why those looks and intimations proclaimed me *overprotective, misguided, a barrier to progress?* Dear Psychiatrist, I really was very confused (didn't Dr Farnstrom say only a month ago, 'He's got to face up to his handicap even if it is painful?'); so confused that I couldn't even collect my thoughts together to construct a question before the conversation moved on . . .

* * *

"Mrs Roberts – the Social Integration Course that was offered by The Heights and refused by you because . . ."

"I did refuse it yes, but not for the reasons stated in the report."

"Well obviously Mrs Roberts you were not going to say, 'I'm sorry Tom can't go because I'm so overprotective!'"

"No, he couldn't go because I couldn't get him there in time."

"And if time hadn't been a factor you'd have been quite happy for him to go?"

"If he'd wanted to, yes."

"And he didn't?"

"No – but I did try very hard to persuade him that it would be a good thing . . . that was until I suddenly realized that, in view of his coming home from school time, I couldn't have got him there for more than the last fifteen minutes."

"Which was convenient – in the circumstances!"

"I can certainly see that is how it might have appeared. However, Miss Godden never told me that's how she was interpreting my words. In fact, though we always *sensed* a strong disapproval, we weren't ever told how we were seen to be failing – till we saw The Heights Report, which of course we weren't supposed to see."

"And which you're not supposed to be discussing yet!"

"No."

"*No!*" the judge reiterated firmly. "Though what I think might be said," he went on, "is that there does, Mrs Roberts, seem to have been a complete failure of communications in these dealings with The Heights; particularly ironic in *your* case because don't I remember, when Tom had scarcely started school, you talked with great eloquence on the importance of language . . ."

. . . training may lead not only to enrichment of speech activity but also to substantial reorganization of the child's whole mental development . . . so does it follow that retardation and

disorganization will result from a child's choosing silence as a coping strategy?

"What we can be quite certain about," said the judge, answering a point put by Mr Shore, "is that Mrs Roberts herself is at completely cross purposes with The Heights while her son, after a very promising start – particularly in the verbal area – has closed-up to the point where language used *of* him features such words as, 'absolutely hopeless', 'will not talk, if he can possibly help it', 'not a thought in his head', 'only talks to start an argument', 'all bottled up like an unexploded bomb'. There do, on the other hand, appear to be some quite eloquent non-verbal statements; most significant to this case being the shoplifting of the chocolate Father Christmas. So, Mrs Roberts, could we please have, in your own words, an explanation of that?"

"Yes – it was a Cry for Help!"

"Those are The Heights' words," said the judge accusingly and checking with his copy of the report, while Mr Grey commented, "Is it not Your Honour, extremely telling that on this *precise* point Mrs Roberts *does* find herself to be in agreement with The Heights?"

"Yes I do see what you mean," said the judge with one more look at the report, "an admission of guilt!" And he actually got up as if to leave . . . "No!" I shouted much louder than I should have done, but I *had* to stop him, "It was a Cry for Help – but not because of overprotectiveness, things like that. It was *bullying!*"

"Bullying!" echoed the judge, "The Heights don't mention that at all".

"I know – that's what worries me, I seemed to spend hours talking about it, in my private sessions with Miss Godden . . ."

. . . but I might as well have spoken to the door.

* * *

Dear Psychiatrist,
I did always realize how difficult it was for you picking up the

pieces in this case. In fact, but for one very unfortunate incident you would not have needed to because the neurological investigations, coinciding with Dr Farnstrom's departure, were to have brought our visits to The Heights to an end – unless anything was found to make further psychiatric assessment advisable. Which of course it wasn't. Then Tom took the chocolate Father Christmas. And once it was realized that the case was to be put through the court we were referred back to you for 'the high regard in which you are held by the magistrates'. They would, we were told, take careful note of your comments and recommendations with consequent benefit to Tom. (There was the feeling too that the probably traumatic experience would be somewhat cushioned for your involvement.)

Tom benefited by only half that chocolate Father Christmas. I know because when I went to release him from police custody the remains were, at some stage, taken from a bag and put on the table that was between us. I remember the still-wrapped head and chest lying there along with other of his possessions, a watch, marble, bus ticket and a little money. There was in fact enough money to have paid for the chocolate Father Christmas. But this of course was a *Cry for Help* – an essential ingredient of which is that the act must be in some way unconventional, (if not necessarily unlawful) in order to attract attention.

Isn't that exactly what I've been doing with this Case History – attempting to get a message across by breaking all sorts of rules and conventions? For I do realize that a judge in Father-Christmas-red is High Court Criminal, and I do realize that no witnesses have been called, nor even the jury.

* * *

The hearing meant a day away from school which pleased Tom. And that seemed a good start, for we really didn't want the experience to be unduly punitive, just enough to make him think.

(He'd been chastened enough at the time by a police sergeant who'd thought that a physical inability to maintain eye contact to be evasive shiftiness – just one of those misconceptions I must let pass for explanations would have been perceived by Tom as worse than the castigation.) Besides, the deed was by this time four months past and things were already much improved as a result of the dog we'd got for him and which had, very obediently, turned out to be the proverbial best friend and confidence booster. Certainly Tom seemed quite relaxed and not noticeably daunted by the forbidding structure of the Magistrates Court. He was even happy to lose himself in a book in the even more forbidding structure of the waiting hall until his name, echoing around, had him leaping to his feet, with us, to cross the floor to the usher who had called. She gave us peremptory instructions on court etiquette as she marshalled us to our seats.

The lay-out of a court is surely designed to command a fitting respect for the law. We – Bill, myself, with Tom in between – sat on a hard bench immediately opposite *the* bench, which was raised three feet or so above us. Another cry from the usher and again we leapt to attention as the three magistrates walked in, silent, stern and grey-suited. They took their high leather-backed seats while higher still hung portraits of former dignitaries, adding to the inscrutable stares.

We were told we might sit, and did, together with other grey figures who were assembled, one almost immediately jumping to his feet again to declare how Tom Roberts had, on a particular day and at a particular time, removed from such-and-such store a chocolate Father Christmas, the aforesaid article . . .

Such a grandiose performance for so petty a crime seemed more fitting a Whitehall Farce, surely even the magistrates . . . but no, the chocolate-Father-Christmas-lifter of today might be the mugger of tomorrow. They kept their steely stares. When that performance was over another grey-suited figure promptly leapt up to say the same thing all over again (he was acting for us I was told later). There were possibly a few exchanges here and we then once more stood to attention, as bidden by an usher, and the magistrates filed out to a side-room to consider The Heights Report.

We relaxed a little. Soon they would understand, perhaps even realize that it might be appropriate to relax a little themselves . . . though I was surprised how long it seemed to be taking for them to appreciate this. 'No one wants to punish him, just make him think' we had been assured at The Heights, 'The case is little more than a formality'. Fifteen minutes went by and still we sat, silently. (We had been told we might talk by an usher who had managed also to convey that we might lose marks if we did so.)

Twenty minutes into our wait and the clerk to the court went into the room that the magistrates had adjourned to, perhaps, we thought, to see if they were ready to return. However, he came back alone, but bearing a piece of paper which he handed to us. It was The Heights Report.

* * *

Dear Psychiatrist,

When I wrote to you following the court hearing my concluding paragraph was, 'We were only given time for one reading of your report so perhaps have not got a balanced view. We should be most grateful if you would let us have a copy so that we could make a more careful study of it'. We did not receive a copy and so have had to continue to rely on our memory of that one reading (which I did, however, commit to paper within three hours of the hearing). I will include relevant bits from my own notes here and apologize for any discrepancies that there might be.

The first paragraph, giving background information on the case, struck me in only one detail and that was the quoting of the IQ established when Tom was four years old (it was, therefore, fifteen points too low). Schools were correctly listed as were the doctors seen, beginning with a completely fair, 'Dr North, paediatrician, supported the family over the first seven years'. We were less happy with, 'Mr and Mrs Roberts embarked upon a course of neurological stimulation for their son but gave it up on finding it not to work'. It then ran on, 'Dr Heckman (psychiatrist) offered help and guidance and Dr Heavens (neurologist) was extremely kind in spending so much time discussing the case with the parents'.

The section on *the parents* followed and this I did read several times. It began, 'Mr Roberts is a quiet man who openly admits to having a bad relationship with his son whom he does not understand'. And it continued, 'Because of Tom's handicap Mrs Roberts has been very overprotective, not allowing him to have friends or to join clubs. This has had an adverse affect on his development and further has led to his solitary excursions to town and ultimately to the shoplifting offence which might be seen as a Cry for Help'.

Your report goes on to list the extent of The Heights' involvement, namely, the monthly meetings with us over the course of a year, two school visits and one to the home to meet Giles and Jill. The Course in Social Integration was mentioned in the context of a service that was offered to meet a specific need but, 'Refused by Mrs Roberts as she is so overprotective'. And *the need for a hobby* which we had voiced was registered, but in words so obviously springing from a report of Miss Godden's that I take the liberty of quoting here her rather fuller comments.

I was shown Miss Godden's report just one month after the court hearing, though it had, in fact, been written immediately following our first visit to The Heights. Miss Godden was remarking on points that I had made in giving the Case History specifically, in this instance, those relating to his poor self-image (following the bullying, ridicule, failure etc.). What I actually said was that such was his fear of failure that he refused to do anything where he might fail. This meant that he had no hobbies and *time hung very heavily*. Then, to emphasize the change that this represented, I added, 'This was certainly not the case in the past! Up to the age of nine or ten, *before* his deep sense of failure set in, he always had some consuming hobby' and I specifically mentioned chess and stamp collecting. I remember being very surprised at the lack of response, for this was my punch line, which usually did hit.

But Miss Godden showed not the slightest reaction, not even to the extent of a raised eyebrow. Neither was anything jotted down. Some time later however, she wrote in the report that I eventually came to see, 'Tom's parents say that he gets easily bored and shows no inclination to follow hobbies. During the conversation they mentioned chess and stamp collecting as hobbies that might be suitable! This strikes me as showing a very poor understanding of Tom's limitations and it is quite possible that unrealistic expectations have been placed upon him both at home and at school thus adding to his deep sense of failure'.

But absolutely nowhere, in either your report or that of Miss Godden, was there any mention of the bullying or of the ridicule which we had spent so long outlining as the chief cause of Tom's unhappiness, lack of confidence and deep sense of failure.

I think you ended, Dear Psychiatrist, with certain recommendations to the magistrates. This section I do not remember at all clearly though of course *you* would be able, if you so wished, to check with the actual report which, I imagine, will now form part of the official Case History.

* * *

An usher ordered, 'Be upstanding for the magistrates' and obediently we stood as again they filed in and solemnly took their high leather-backed seats. Were the stares still inscrutable or were they now quite directed . . . ? "Mr and Mrs Roberts, do you have anything that you would like to say?"

Did we have anything that we would like to say! We were so bursting with words, words, words . . .

Words *were* the key and yet, if we said what we would like to have said, the case might have been adjourned pending further investigations . . . and we really didn't want Tom to have to return. "No, thank you no, we have nothing to say."

"Very well. *Tom*, I have to tell you that if you steal anything again you might be taken away from home and put into care. Do you understand? Yes? And Mr and Mrs Roberts you will please pay thirty five pence to the solicitor representing the offended store – that being the price of the chocolate Father Christmas that Tom took."

And then we were free to go.

7th May

Dear Psychiatrist,

The court case is now over.

We wonder whether you are aware that reports that you write for the direction of the magistrates are handed to parents to read? We are very disturbed by many of your comments. Please would it be possible to have one more consultation to put our point of view?

POSTSCRIPT

Tom left school when he was sixteen and did not suffer bullying again. As a result his tremor gradually lessened until – a year or so later – it was barely noticeable. It took a lot longer for his confidence to return, possibly because employment opportunities were so poor. He was, however, good at finding part-time jobs (door-to-door salesman, brass cleaning, gardening), which he did completely satisfactorily. It was around this time that his great love of cycling developed and he began making a very thorough exploration of the countryside within a fifty mile radius of our house (he might cycle anything up to one hundred and fifty miles in a day). By far his greatest love and interest, however, remained his Golden Labrador dog.

The first (full-time) work that really caught his imagination was helping to create a wildlife garden for hospital patients on a locally sponsored training scheme. Sadly the money ran out before the project was completed, but he immediately began writing letters to potential employers and was quickly successful in getting a job as a groundsman at a college sports-ground. Now his confidence really returned, and with it all those qualities that I once feared lost; humour, communicativeness, (though he remained a very private person) thoughtfulness – in the widest sense of that word. He developed a very concerned interest in world wildlife and environmental issues, becoming actively involved in fund-raising events, in collecting names for various petitions and in writing to MPs on a wide variety of matters (seal culling, halon gas use, road widening schemes etc.). He also took part in a number of countryside conservation working weekends and holidays. Meanwhile, he kept up his cycling pursuits, touring in this country and abroad (before visiting Germany he did a year's course in German).

Three years into his job as a groundsman (he did five and a half years in all) he felt that he would like more challenging work and again began enquiring about openings in either gardening or woodland management. This time he was not lucky and so began thinking about training in these fields. (The death of his dog at Christmas 1993, although very sad, at least freed him to pursue a course away from home.)

In 1994 he was successful in gaining a place on a conservation/land management course at an agricultural college in the North Midlands. He started on 19th September and in weekly telephone conversations with him I learned that the course was going well, his fellow students were, 'A great lot' and his digs good. It was clear he was working hard both at his studies and also at weekends on conservation work schemes. On 29th October he returned home for a week's half term break and the whole family (including a new niece and nephew) came to spend the first weekend with him. The rest of the week was uneventfully normal, he did some course work, was his usual industrious and good-natured self around the house and garden.

On 6th November – the day he was due to return to college – he committed suicide.

In a long and quite exceptionally thoughtful letter that he left for us, Tom was chiefly concerned to apologize for the hurt he was going to cause, to express affection for his family, to explain his state of mind, and to try to relieve anyone of any feeling of guilt they might have had. He said he was happy at home and at college (all our contacts with the college confirm this – he was well liked and his work was completely satisfactory). He could even recognize that the last seven years had been good. However, he just could not forgive himself for the ten years before that (ages 10-20). He mentions negative attitudes, wasting opportunities and time, failing to try his hardest to achieve. Such regrets apparently built up to a turmoil that he found quite unbearable to live with. And because he told no one, no one could say, 'It wasn't your fault! Besides, the really important thing is that you *are* achieving now'.

* * *

Since Tom's death we have learned that he almost certainly suffered from Asperger Syndrome, which we understand to be a very mild form of Autism. Though we ourselves would have been enormously helped had *someone* given us this diagnosis when he was a child, it is just possible that he did better for not being labelled.

Notes

1. A term used since the Education Act 1981 to describe any child needing special educational help (of whatever description) during all or part of his or her schooling. (In that he started school before 1981 Tom was never officially classed a special needs child. I have used the term knowing it to be the one currently preferred.)
2. This would have been a school for educationally subnormal (ESN) children.
3. A person working under the class teacher's direction, having no teaching qualifications her or himself.
4. The system that operated until the Education Act 1981, after which schools were encouraged to adopt a more flexible policy towards integrating Special Needs Children into ordinary classes.
5. Several years later I realised that the word *perseverance* should perhaps have been *perseveration*, which I understand to mean the repeated use of a response (thought, word, action) which was successful in the past but which is no longer appropriate. Thus it will prevent progression to the next stage.
6. Speech and the Development of Mental Processes in the Child by A.R. Luria and F. la Yudovich.
7. Electroencephalogram.
8. I am not actually giving the word he used for over-protectiveness as this might be to identify the doctor.
9. This was before schools were encouraged (or inclined) to adopt anti-bullying policies. At the schools that Tom went to, teachers aimed to stop bullying in the classroom but tended to consider it fairly inevitable in the playground.
10. Warnock Report 1978 on Children with Special Educational Needs, estimated then to be 20% of the school population, 2% of whom would need help in special schools the remaining 18% in mainstream education.
11. A school doctor attempted this and I think rather added to Tom's unease regarding the matter.
12. This request followed his watching, a year previously, a Sealed Knot re-enaction of the Battle of Edgehill.
13. A pretence of helplessness in order to avoid the risk of failure.